"The way to enjoy Venice is to follow the example of these people and make the most of simple pleasures."

Henry James

VENICE

FOUR SEASONS
OF HOME
COOKING

✳

RUSSELL NORMAN

Photography by Jenny Zarins

RIZZOLI
NEW YORK

New York · Paris · London · Milan

First published in the United States of America in 2018 by
Rizzoli International Publications, Inc.
300 Park Avenue South
New York, NY 10010
www.rizzoliusa.com

Originally published in the United Kingdom in 2018 by
Fig Tree, a division of Penguin Random House UK

2018 2019 2020 2021 / 10 9 8 7 6 5 4 3 2 1

ISBN: 978-0-8478-6318-1

Library of Congress Control Number: 2018940564

Printed in Germany

CONTENTS

PROLOGUE

Venice, August 1986

It is late. I am sitting with friends outside a restaurant in Giardini, a residential neighborhood on the eastern edge of Venice. The night sky still glows pink from the dying day, and swifts wheel and chirp in the warm air above us.

I catch the waiter's eye and hold up our empty wine jug. I really don't want this night to end. It is my last day in the city. I have spent three weeks here and tomorrow I must travel back to England.

Venice bewitches. Like many before me, I have been seduced by its art, architecture, poetry, and beauty. But there is something else. As I pack my bags and prepare to catch the waterbus to the train station, I sense unfinished business: it's the neighborhood that's got me, not the city.

Traveling along the Grand Canal, I know I will be back. But what I don't realize is that, despite many trips to Venice over the coming decades, it will take me thirty years to return to Giardini.

INTRODUCTION

One of the great pleasures of foreign travel is exploring food markets, ogling butchers' windows, marveling at the variety of ingredients and produce. One of the great frustrations, however, is not being able to buy it all, take it home, and cook. Hotels, as convenient and pleasurable as they are, do not have en suite kitchens, so my natural instincts as an amateur chef and jobbing restaurateur are continually thwarted.

Nowhere have I felt this more keenly than in Venice. My connection with the city is both personal and professional, and in recent years the frequency of my visits has increased. This has only served to emphasize the frustration. My hotel of choice for several years has been a small, humble, and dilapidated *pensione*, a guesthouse on the southern tip of Dorsoduro, perched on the edge of the Giudecca Canal. It is beautiful in the manner of so much of Venice, having a faded elegance and an easy charm that has certainly helped me to feel at one with my surroundings. But, apart from eating in restaurants and, when I am particularly fortunate, in friends' houses, my culinary connectedness has faltered. I have only ever been able to eat in the city like a tourist or as a houseguest. I have never been able to go to the markets in the morning, engage with the stallholders, choose the inkiest cuttlefish or the plumpest peaches, the brightest sardines or the purplest artichokes, and march home to prepare the evening meal. In other words, I've never been able to cook like a Venetian.

A couple of years ago I found myself back in the residential neighborhood of Giardini. It was one of those glorious evenings that only Venice can deliver: expansive bruised skies with silhouetted bell towers on the horizon, lights from boats reflected on the surface of the lagoon, the sound of water lapping on the *fondamenta*. I was transported back thirty years and was overcome with a disorienting sense of déjà vu.

Later, over a simple supper of risotto in a Venetian friend's kitchen, I had a bit of an epiphany. What would it be like to live and write in one of the most visited cities in the world and experience it like a local? Go to the same markets, buy the same cuts of meat, choose the same fish and seafood, carry home the same vegetables, and effectively immerse oneself in the gastronomic heart of one of the least known and most misunderstood food cultures in Europe? Additionally, knowing what I did about the way Venetians celebrate seasonal ingredients and the dramatically changing nature of the markets, month to month, I reckoned that if I were to take on that challenge I would need to write about buying, preparing, cooking, and eating *in real time*, over the course of four seasons, in a real Venetian kitchen.

The location of this realization was significant. Much has been written about those Venetian classics found in the city's handful of excellent restaurants (and even in many of the poor ones, too) and in the growing number of cookery books that champion the food of the region. Fewer column inches, however, have been devoted to the genuine *home cooking* of Venice, the sort I was experiencing that evening in Giardini.

The difference between home cooking and restaurant food is often just a question of attitude. The former is heartfelt and generous, born of love, warmth, tradition, and a sense of abundance. The latter counts precision, consistency, and expertise among its virtues. Not being a professional chef myself, I have always had a preference for home cooking, holding gingham-aproned grandmothers in far higher esteem than white-jacketed pros. Along with the honesty you find in a domestic kitchen, you will often discover a startling absence of written recipes, many existing only in the memory of the home cook. It is this oral tradition, with family favorites passed down verbally from generation to generation, that I hoped would form the basis of my exploration, too.

So, my adventure begins in October, a beautiful month in Venice when the days can still be as warm as toast and the markets are at that beguiling threshold between summer and autumn, meaning you can still get wonderful tomatoes but you also see the first radicchio and pumpkins coming from Chioggia and rural Veneto. I have rented a small apartment in a narrow street that forms part of the residential grid just north of the gardens at Giardini. There is a communal altar in the tiny open courtyard where brightly painted mannequins of Jesus Christ and the Virgin keep an eye on the close-knit community. Candles are lit in the evenings and sometimes my new neighbors come out of their houses and sing songs of thanks and praise.

The apartment is humble and sparsely furnished but has a glorious terrazzo floor, bare brick walls in the kitchen, and a balcony wide enough to take a single chair. What more could I ask for? As long as I have an outside spot to sit in the sun and shell fresh peas, I know I will be happy. Importantly, I am very close to Via Garibaldi, the main shopping street of the neighborhood. In my immediate vicinity, there are three greengrocers (one of whom trades from a floating barge), three butchers, two fishmongers, a bakery, an *enoteca*, and a domestic hardware store specializing in plastic buckets, pegs, and discounted shampoo. Further afield are a small supermarket, a couple of spritz bars, and the local communist club.

Via Garibaldi is simply beautiful. It runs northeast to southwest, so from mid-morning to late afternoon the sun has nowhere to go other than directly along its tall terraced sides and across the cambered Istrian paving stones. It is a *rio terra*, in other words, a canal that has been paved over. You can still see the shape of the original waterway and only a small leap of imagination is required to picture it as it once was, gondolas sailing past, sunlight glinting.

As far as the traders and stallholders are concerned, I quickly identify my allies. For fish you go to Delfino, located close to where the Sant'Anna Canal starts. It's a lively place with a permanent backdrop of reggae music playing on a tinny beatbox, but the seafood is good. Maurizio and Nicola are the unlikeliest fishmongers and you get a good dose of banter with everything you buy. For fruit and vegetables it's Stefano, in Campiello Caboto. He employs a couple of cheeky chaps who flirt outrageously with the (mostly) elderly female clientele. Not only do they get away with it but, judging by the crowds, they are as popular as the *piselli* and *puntarelle*. The *enoteca*, like many across the city, simply fills your empty plastic water bottles with the wine of your choice for a few euros. Stefania, a local character with a big voice, runs the place with the efficiency of a sergeant-major. And for meat, I head back to the *macelleria* on the corner of Calle de le Ancore. It is the butcher's shop with the longest lines—always an encouraging sign. One could argue that Italian cooking is more about good shopping than good technique. Of course, you need to have a certain level of competence in the kitchen, but if the ingredients are excellent to start with, then you have to do less to them.

With my base established and my kitchen outfitted with only the most rudimentary equipment, I am able to begin the serious business of stalking my neighbors. I follow them to the markets, ambushing them with questions in my pidgin Italian (*"Mi scusi, signora, cosa farai con questi ingredienti?"*), and then I go home to make the dish myself. It is a particularly rewarding way to get to know a region's food culture and its traditions. What I also discover, of course, as well as the fastidious seasonal discipline of these home cooks, is that they borrow freely from other parts of Italy. Dishes from Puglia, Sicily, Tuscany, Lombardy, and Emilia-Romagna appear with frequency and with no sense of disloyalty nor any less pride. In fact, it transpires that some locals believe recipes made famous in other regions were originally stolen from Venice in the first place. (Mrs. Povinelli, in particular, insists that the meat *ragù* the world associates so closely with Bologna was ripped off from the ancient Venetian recipe for *secoe*.)

This book charts the culinary journey I made over the course of fourteen months in that scruffy apartment in Giardini. Some of the recipes are traditional, some put together from fragmented conversations with ninety-year-old great-grandmothers, some given to me by professional Venetian chefs whom I have befriended, others from enthusiastic amateurs who, once they got wind of my project, would collar me and tell me I absolutely *must* include their mother's recipe for *this* or their grandfather's version of *that*. A few of the dishes in these pages are regional impostors, and I make no excuse for that. This is home cooking, with all the idiosyncrasies and aberrations that come with it. Venice has, over the centuries, occupied and been occupied, and the influences of other regions on its cuisine are there to see and taste at every turn.

There was, for me, a compelling reason to follow the seasons and to divide the recipes into those four categories. They are so distinct, and the markets so different at the four meteorological junctions of the year, that the food on family tables reflects that. Since I was living, shopping, cooking, and writing in real time, it seemed only sensible to shape the book in real time, too. And how apt that the birthplace of Antonio Vivaldi should also be the scene for my own *Quattro Stagioni*.

But, above all else, I believe this collection is a snapshot of the food cooked and eaten by real Venetians, a population that is dwindling at a rate of one thousand inhabitants a year. No one really knows the true consequences for Venice if this decline continues, but as long as those remaining residents continue to cook and eat with such passion and sense of pride, there is a small part of the unique character and culture of the city that will always survive.

BROCCOLI AND ANCHOVY CROSTINI • SARDINE "TONGUES" • CASTRAURE AND PARMESAN SALAD • WARM SALAD OF LAMB, MINT, AND NEW POTATO • GRILLED ASPARAGUS, GOAT'S CURD, AND SPECK BRUSCHETTA • FRIED SAGE LEAVES • WATERCRESS, BROAD BEAN, PECORINO, AND PEA SHOOT SALAD • WILD GARLIC SOUP • BABY ARTICHOKE RISOTTO • VENETIAN RICE AND PEAS • SPAGHETTI WITH ONIONS • CRAB AND CHILE LINGUINE • SPAGHETTI WITH CLAMS, BOTTARGA, AND WHIPPED PEAS • SAUSAGE AND EGG BUCATINI • SMALL GNOCCHI WITH BABY SQUID AND CINNAMON • GRILLED SPRING VEGETABLE PIZZA • RED ONION PIZZA • FRITTATA WITH PRAWNS AND DILL • JOHN DORY WITH ASPARAGUS AND BASIL • MACKEREL CAPONATA • VIGNOLE • BRAISED PEAS WITH BASIL • ESPRESSO MARTINI • PINZA • ZALETI • TOBLERONE ZABAIONE • SMALL WILD STRAWBERRIES WITH TARRAGON

S P R I N G

"The way to happiness is to think no further ahead than lunch or dinner."

Stephen Bayley (after Sydney Smith)

I spend much of my time in search of the simple, and my day will usually begin with thoughts of food. I am often drawn to the market, as if in the embrace of a powerful tractor beam, by the promise of a new ingredient, or the delivery of a particularly splendid batch of some familiar ones.

To say that Italian cooking starts with the ingredient would be a significant understatement. Italian cooking *is* the ingredient. From Sicily in the hot, dry south to Alto Adige in the verdant, temperate north, the food philosophy is the same: less is more. I find regional differences are not so much about technique in the kitchen, but rather to do with variations in what's available. Generally speaking, it is the peasant tradition of simplicity that pervades and persists. And necessity tends to be mother of invention with many of Italy's iconic dishes: panzanella, the vibrant Tuscan salad, is a thrillingly simple and delicious way to deal with a glut of tomatoes and a stash of stale bread. Vignole, from Lazio and Umbria, is a riot of springtime greenery, the only sensible way to cope with the abundance of peas, artichokes, and chard at that time of year.

Spring takes me out of the house earlier every day and on a much more frequent basis. It's a cliché, I know, but the sense of new life and rebirth is visible everywhere, even in a city made of marble and stone. But often I crave more bucolic surroundings, and as lovely as the generous grassy square in front of the church of San Pietro di Castello is, my English sensibilities get the better of me and I start planning my first visit of the year to my favorite Venetian island.

A short trip on the number 13 vaporetto takes me over the most peaceful part of the lagoon to the island of Sant'Erasmo, a place of surprising calm and tranquility. It is a geographical miracle—a long, narrow stretch of land with the Adriatic along one flank and the brackish lagoon on the other. How anything survives here is a wonder, yet much of the greengrocery you find in Rialto Market and on the fruit and veg barges across the city comes from the island. Furthermore, the fruit produce grown in its farms and gardens is revered above anything from other areas of Italy. This is partly a matter of local pride and partly because the quality is superb.

I remember the first time I visited. I was going to see Michel Thoulouze, a French ex-pat who bought a house and land on Sant'Erasmo several decades ago and decided to plant Malvasia and Vermentino vines. He now makes one of the only wines produced entirely in the lagoon. He also keeps Padovana chickens, those peculiar poultry with heads like elaborate feather dusters. After spending an hour or two with Michel, I went for a very long walk. The vineyards gave way to fields of purple artichokes, allotments growing zucchini, peas, asparagus, chard. The sense of lush fertility is quite remarkable.

As I sailed back to Venice on an almost empty vaporetto, I did so with a renewed sense of admiration for a city that has evolved with a substantial degree of self-sufficiency, using available resources in a very similar manner to the kitchen philosophy of its home cooks.

While Sant'Erasmo is characterized by silence and serenity, Rialto Market could not be more different. It is raucous, brash, frenetic, and noisy. But it is a thrilling place that makes you feel you are in the beating cultural and culinary heart of the city. On busy mornings, it really can be difficult to move, and even when you are able to dodge the tourists, traders, and shoppers, you'll not get up a pace much faster than the *bovoletti* snails that crawl out of the overflowing buckets near the fish stalls.

I experienced quite a commotion one early spring day, March 8, as it happens, when the first soft-shell crabs of the season arrived. With such a small window of opportunity to catch these *moeche* as they are moulting, they are rare and eye-wateringly expensive. But I feel just as much excitement when I spot a newcomer of any ilk. I remember seeing *telline* clams for the first time, tiny smooth bivalves no bigger than your fingernail. I bought two kilos on the spot without much of an idea what I was going to do with them. I needn't have worried. They were perfect briefly sautéed with olive oil, salt, garlic, and chopped parsley.

I love the sideshows around the market, too. There's a broad-shouldered fellow named Tomas who spends hours every day cutting the leaves from artichokes, trimming the stalk back, and carving out the heart, or *fondo*, before throwing it into a huge tub of acidulated water with the hundreds of others. These are then sold at a premium, all the hard work done for you. And there's the silent, brooding chap who finds shade to set up his table where he decapitates, disembowels and butterflies one tiny sardine after another, using only his thumbnails, neatly laying them out on a sheet in front of him, his hands and forearms drenched in blood up to the elbow. These little spatchcocked fish are known as sardine "tongues" and they are delicious in a light batter, swiftly fried (recipe on page 22).

Spring is the season when Venice leaps out of the dark, cold months of January and February and seems to say, "Life is here, let's rejoice." That sense of celebration and rebirth is nowhere more evident than in the markets, in the ingredients, in recipes, and in the city's home cooking.

BROCCOLI *and* ANCHOVY CROSTINI

A bar snack for 4

One beautifully sunny spring afternoon, the food writer and Venice resident Anna Gilchrist took me to a new wine bar near the Scuola Grande di San Rocco. I spotted a little cichèto behind the counter that I hadn't come across before, and this is my version of it.

I've never considered broccoli prepared any other way than very fresh, briefly boiled, or steamed and served with lots of salt. I've always associated soft, pulpy broccoli with school dinners. But here, mashed, with the salty, tangy anchovies, it's a different story. Perfect with a pre-prandial Campari and soda.

½ a French baguette
2 cups broccoli florets
flaky sea salt
freshly ground black pepper
2 (2-ounce) cans of anchovies
½ a lemon

Slice the baguette on an angle to create 8 elliptical discs ½ inch thick. Lay them on a baking sheet and toast them lightly under a broiler for a few minutes each side, until golden brown. Set aside.

Bring a large saucepan of salted water to a boil and cook the broccoli florets until quite soft but not too watery and mushy, about 6 minutes, depending on the size of the florets. Drain, rinse under cold running water, drain thoroughly again, then transfer to a large mixing bowl. Crunch over a generous amount of salt flakes and a twist of black pepper, then, using a potato masher, roughly mash the broccoli into a thick paste. Leave to stand for a minute or two.

Open the cans of anchovies and separate the fish. There are normally 8 to 10 fillets per 2-ounce can. Roughly chop half of them and add to the broccoli. Mix thoroughly.

Spoon an equal amount of the broccoli/anchovy mix over the eight peices of toast, drape over a single anchovy lengthwise, add a twist of black pepper and a few drops of lemon juice, and serve as a bar snack.

SARDINE "TONGUES"

For 4, as a starter

The name of this dish comes from the shape of the tiny butterflied sardine cutlets. The headless, gutted little fillets still retain their tails but in their splayed state look vaguely like tongues. These are lovely as a starter on individual plates, but also excellent on a large serving tray as canapés.

16 sardines, gutted, filleted, and decapitated
1½ cups "00" flour, seasoned
1 large egg, beaten
7 ounces panko breadcrumbs
4¼ cups vegetable oil, for deep-frying
1 lemon, quartered
fine salt

Wash the sardines under cold running water and thoroughly dry. Take a very sharp knife and cut the belly side right down to the tail. Now push the two flanks of each fish to the side to create 16 cutlets with all the tails still intact.

Put the salted flour onto a large plate, the beaten egg into a bowl, and the breadcrumbs onto a plate, and line all three up like a factory production line.

Heat the oil in a large saucepan to around 375°F/190°C. You can test this by dropping a cube of bread into the pan—it should turn light brown in about 20 seconds.

Lightly coat each cutlet in flour, shake off. Dip in the egg, shake off. Then coat in breadcrumbs. Deep-fry in batches for around 90 seconds, until golden brown, and drain on paper towels.

Serve immediately, while hot, with a wedge of lemon and a pinch more fine salt.

CASTRAURE *and* PARMESAN SALAD

For 4

Here is a salad that Venetians enjoy for a few brief weeks in late April and early May, when the first small artichoke buds appear in the farms of Sant'Erasmo. The *castraure* are so-called because the plant is castrated to allow the secondary artichokes to flourish (these are called *botoli*). Since it is rare to find *castraure* anywhere other than northern Italy, the only time I make this outside Venice is when I have packed my hand luggage with them on trips back to London. This is a recipe to attempt when you've been on a spring trip and you want to bring back a unique flavor of the region.

Because the main ingredient is so delicate, it is important to choose very soft and herby salad leaves. These are available at farmers' market stalls by the bagful. You can also use a supermarket bag of the best quality delicate salad leaves you can find.

16 castraure artichokes
1 tablespoon and 1 teaspoon of lemon juice
4¼ ounces excellent-quality aged Parmesan
¼ cup extra virgin olive oil

flaky sea salt
10½ ounces very delicate, small mixed salad
 leaves, washed and thoroughly dried
freshly ground black pepper

Trim the artichokes of their long stalks up to the base of the bulb. Remove the hard, outer purple leaves until you get to the softer, pale yellow ones. Don't get carried away—*castraure* have no chokes, so you need to be left with a walnut-sized vegetable. Using a very sharp knife, slice the artichokes very thinly indeed and drop them into a small bowl of cold water to which you have added a teaspoon of lemon juice.

Using a speed peeler, or, even better, a truffle slicer on a medium/fine setting, carefully shave the largest intact sheets you can from your block of Parmesan. Set aside.

Take a very large mixing bowl and pour in half the olive oil, half the remaining lemon juice, and a few good pinches of salt. Drain and pat dry the sliced *castraure*, then add them to the mixing bowl and turn several times very carefully with your hand. Now add the salad leaves and the remaining oil and lemon juice and, once again, carefully turn over with your hand, making sure you don't fold or bruise the leaves. Finally, add the Parmesan shavings and turn over again, as delicately as you can so that the slices don't crumble and break up.

Evenly distribute the salad on four large plates, still using your hand and still being as gentle as possible. The artichokes will naturally have migrated to the bottom of the mixing bowl with the shaved Parmesan, so carefully divide the spoils equally, scattering them on top of each plate, and finish with a twist of black pepper.

Serve with a glass of crisp white wine and crusty bread.

WARM SALAD OF LAMB, MINT, *and* NEW POTATO

For 4

As recently as last century, the *campi* of Venice were small grassy fields with livestock. It is quite amusing to imagine sheep grazing among the churches and palaces, but unsurprising, therefore, to find more than a smattering of meat recipes in the canon. The old abattoir in the westernmost reaches of Cannaregio, now defunct, would have satisfied most of the carnivorous cravings of Venetians, but now the local butchers are supplied from the farms of mainland Veneto. Lamb is particularly tender from the foothills of the Dolomites.

This delicious salad must be served warm, since cooked lamb does have a tendency toward clagginess when cold. A little sugar in the dressing intensifies the flavor of the mint and keeps the dish firmly within the boundaries of spring.

7 ounces very small new potatoes	*½ a clove of garlic, peeled and finely*
5 tablespoons extra virgin olive oil	* chopped*
14 ounces lean lamb loin	*a handful of mint leaves, finely shredded*
flaky sea salt	*2 teaspoons Dijon mustard*
freshly ground black pepper	*1 teaspoon superfine sugar*
1 tablespoon red wine vinegar	*1 pound lamb's leaf lettuce*

Bring a large pot of salted water to a boil and cook the new potatoes for about 15 minutes. If they are tiny, leave them whole. If they are larger, cut them in half. Drain them and cover with a damp cloth until they are needed.

Meanwhile, preheat the oven to 350°F/180°C. Take an ovenproof heavy-bottomed frying pan and heat a tablespoon of the olive oil over a high flame. Liberally season the lamb joint with salt and pepper and sear it on all sides in the pan until browned. Transfer to the oven and roast for about 25 minutes, turning once. Remove, place on a wooden board and cover with foil. Allow to rest for 15 minutes.

While the meat is resting, make the dressing. Put the remaining olive oil, red wine vinegar, garlic, mint, and mustard into a jam jar with a tightly fitting lid. Add a pinch of salt, the sugar, and a twist of black pepper, then secure the lid firmly and shake vigorously over the sink for 30 seconds until smooth, silky, and emulsified. Taste and adjust the seasoning if necessary.

Place the lamb's leaf in a large mixing bowl, and add the cooked potatoes. Slice the lamb thinly, around ¼ inch, tossing the slices into the mixing bowl. Finally, add enough of the dressing to just coat the ingredients and turn over several times with your hand. Serve on wide plates and finish with a twist of black pepper.

GRILLED ASPARAGUS, GOAT'S CURD, *and* SPECK BRUSCHETTA

For 4

The transformative qualities of direct heat and flame, though well known to fans of grilling, are less common in the domestic kitchen. For this reason, I do like to get my grill pan out on occasion, not just for the tang of charring, but also the beautiful grill lines on those ingredients that are subjected to the smoking hot, ribbed cooking surface.

This dish occurred to me quite unexpectedly one morning at the fruit and veg barge on Via Garibaldi, simply because the asparagus had been displayed next to the pea shoots. The results were rather lovely. Speck is a delicious, lightly smoked prosciutto from Alto Adige, and you need to ask for it to be sliced so thinly that light passes through it when you hold a slice up to the window.

8 medium asparagus spears, woody ends removed
extra virgin olive oil
flaky sea salt
4 slices of decent sourdough, ¾ inch thick

1 clove of garlic, peeled
4 large slices of speck, very thinly sliced
5¼ ounces goat's curd
a handful of pea shoots
freshly ground black pepper

If your asparagus spears are more than ½ inch thick, you must blanch them first. Bring a large pan of salted water to a boil, put the asparagus in, and cook for 2 to 3 minutes maximum. Drain and plunge the spears into cold water for a minute, then dry and set aside. If your asparagus are more slender, you don't need to prepare them, other than removing the woody stalk ends in both cases.

Take the grill pan and rub the entire cooking surface with a little olive oil. Place over high heat. Take the asparagus spears and coat with olive oil, using your hands. Lay them on the grill pan and crunch over some flakes of salt. After a couple of minutes, carefully turn them over using kitchen tongs and do the same on all sides until you have nice, defined grill lines. Cut the spears at an angle into 1½ inch long pieces. Set aside.

Rub a little olive oil over both sides of each slice of bread and lay them on the hot grill. A couple of minutes on each side should give you nice dark grill marks on the bread, too.

Slice the garlic clove in half and gently rub the cut edge over one side of each slice of sourdough. Carefully lay on the slices of speck, with a few folds to create some height. Crumble over the goat's curd. Evenly distribute the asparagus pieces and scatter over the pea shoots.

Finally, add a pinch of salt and a twist of black pepper, finishing with a drizzle of olive oil.

FRIED SAGE LEAVES

A small snack for a small gathering

Sometimes the simplest things are capable of giving the greatest pleasure. A single sage leaf coated in a light batter and fried briefly until crisp and brittle may not sound like the pinnacle of culinary achievement, but there is an understated elegance to this little confection that belies its simplicity.

Sage has a potent flavor, intensified by the frying process. I will often make a batch of these snacks to accompany a pre-prandial cocktail, and there is nothing better for that purpose than an extremely cold, extremely dry Gin Martini. You can find my recipe on page 136.

¾ cup plus 1 tablespoon plain flour
1 large egg, beaten
1 cup cold carbonated water
40 sage leaves, washed and dried
4¼ cups vegetable oil, for deep-frying
fine salt

Put the flour into a large mixing bowl and add the egg. Beat together with a wooden spoon, then very slowly add the water, all the while mixing with the spoon. Continue until you have a smooth, creamy, dense mixture, just like pancake batter.

Heat the oil to 375°F/190°C in a large saucepan. You can test this by dropping a small cube of white bread into the oil—it should turn golden brown in 20 seconds. Carefully submerge the sage leaves in the batter, then drop them individually (making sure they do not clump) in small batches into the oil. When they are crisp and golden, remove them with a slotted spoon and lay them on a double sheet of paper towels. Sprinkle with fine salt and serve immediately.

WATERCRESS, BROAD BEAN, PECORINO, *and* PEA SHOOT SALAD

For 4

I find that there are substantial variations in the size of watercress leaves. Sometimes the plant is coarse and dark with very thick stalks, and while these varieties are wonderfully intense and peppery, they do not make for great salads. So you need to seek out the very delicate, herby version with small leaves and pale stalks. When dressing this salad, use your hands to turn over the ingredients, not salad servers, and be as gentle and as careful as you can. You really must try not to bruise or crease the leaves; you want them to stand springy and proud on the plate.

a large handful of golden raisins
2¼ pounds fresh broad (fava) beans in their
*   pods, podded to yield 9 ounces beans*
10½ ounces baby watercress leaves
extra virgin olive oil

the zest and juice of ½ a lemon
flaky sea salt
a large handful of pea shoots
3½ ounces Pecorino Romano, shaved
freshly ground black pepper

Put the raisins into a bowl of cold water and soak for half an hour. Drain and pat dry.

Meanwhile, pod the broad beans and put them into a large pan of boiling water for 2 minutes. Drain and rinse under a cold running tap, then set aside.

Remove and discard all the thickest stalks from the watercress leaves, then wash and dry using a salad spinner.

Take the broad beans and remove the inner green pulses from the white membranes by piercing them with your thumbnail and pushing the bean through. (This is one of the most satisfying and therapeutic kitchen jobs I know.)

Take a very large mixing bowl and add the broad beans, watercress, and raisins. Drizzle with a couple of tablespoons of olive oil, add the lemon juice, and a few pinches of salt, and gently turn over a few times with your hands. Finally, add the pea shoots and the lemon zest, carefully turn over once more and divide equally between four large plates. Scatter over the shaved Pecorino, finish with a twist of black pepper, and serve.

WILD GARLIC SOUP

For 4

Wild garlic is an ingredient that I adore when I am in England in the spring months. It grows abundantly in the forests of Kent and Sussex. I was delighted, therefore, to come across it one late March morning at the Rialto Market, labeled as *aglio trigano*. The leaves were smaller and slightly triangular in shape, but it had the same distinctive aroma. In a rare example of reverse migration, I have made this soup for my Venetian friends and they adore it.

Wild garlic has a subtle flavor, not at all like the bulb, and a rather shockingly intense color. I don't think there is anything else as thrillingly green as wild garlic soup. It is a wonderful herby harbinger of spring.

1 large floury potato, peeled and quartered
extra virgin olive oil
a small bunch of scallions, chopped
1 celery stalk, chopped
flaky sea salt

10½ ounces wild garlic, washed and
    thoroughly drained
6⅓ cups vegetable stock (see page 304)
crème fraîche

Bring a small pot of water to a boil. Add the potato and cook for about 12 minutes, then drain and set aside. Meanwhile, warm a glug of olive oil in a large pot over medium heat, and gently sauté the scallion and celery with a couple of very good pinches of salt for about 12 minutes, until soft and glossy, making sure they do not color.

Sort through the washed garlic leaves to remove any impostors—ivy tends to be the most common culprit—and set aside a handful of the delicate white flowers. Add the wild garlic to the sautéed scallions and celery, along with the potato pieces and a ladleful of stock. Stir several times, add a few more pinches of salt, then cover and cook for 3 to 5 minutes. Remove the lid, add the rest of the stock, bring to a boil, then simmer over low heat for an additional 5 minutes, stirring frequently.

Remove from the heat and transfer to a blender. Whiz for a minute to ensure everything is reduced to a very smooth and velvety consistency. You may need to do this in batches. Transfer back to the large saucepan, bring to a gentle simmer, test the seasoning, and adjust if necessary. Stir in 2 tablespoons of crème fraîche, then remove from the heat and place the pan in the middle of the table. It is so stunningly green you want everyone to see it in all its vibrant glory.

Serve in warmed bowls with an extra little dollop of crème fraîche if you like, a scattering of the retained white flowers, and plenty of crusty bread.

Shopping—a morning ritual

Venice's bells are a reassuring daily soundtrack, their surprising harmonics often rooting me to the spot as I try to pick out the musical notes. One warm April day a few years ago, I went for a long walk with a digital tuning fork and compiled a short catalogue of churches and their bells. (I try to make my own fun.) After a cup of coffee from my battered, stovetop Bialetti, I set out to Via Garibaldi, my local shopping street.

Most residents pull standard-issue wheeled shopping baskets behind them when they shop. They are perfect for navigating narrow alleyways and small bridges and easily hold all the groceries needed for a day's cooking for a large family. Mine is dark red with black wheels and a brown plastic handle, and I'm very fond of it.

The first thing I do is head for Alla Rampa for my second coffee of the day. I am always bemused by the unwritten rules and the way locals do things one way while tourists do them another. One should always drink coffee standing *"al banco"*—at the bar. Only tourists sit. Never order a milky coffee, and certainly not after 12 noon. If you ask for a "latte"' you'll get a glass of milk. *Caffè macchiato* is the normal form, maybe with a little biscuit or, in January and February, *fritole*—Venetian doughnuts.

Just outside Alla Rampa is the greengrocer's barge, a neighborhood meeting point as well as the place you buy your vegetables. (I usually head a block away, to Campiello Caboto, and buy my produce from Stefano Tommasi, but the gossip is better at the barge.) It is here that I will often hold back and look at what the locals are buying before I make up my mind. It's an excellent tactic and a great way to learn from those genuine home cooks.

I have, on many occasions, followed a particular neighbor to see exactly what she buys and then quizzed her about what she's going to make. This way I have made friends with Mrs. Povinelli and Mrs. Scarpa, both inspirational home cooks with a wide and varied repertoire of dishes from Venice, the Veneto, and beyond.

After visiting the fishmonger and the butcher, there is only time to perhaps buy a newspaper before getting home to refrigerate the morning's hoard. The newsagent is an important social hub, too. In other parts of Venice you will still find the glorious nineteenth-century circular steel and zinc booths selling magazines, newspapers, and maps for tourists. (There is a particularly beautiful example outside the Accademia Gallery, and a rather austere one in Campo Sta Maria Formosa displaying an unambiguous message for any tourists who are even thinking about asking for directions—see photo on page 6.) Here on Via Garibaldi it's the tobacconist and lotto shop that serve a similar purpose, and you will often witness a morning version of the *passeggiata*—neighbours gossiping and catching up, complaining and remonstrating—all part of the Venetian way.

BABY ARTICHOKE RISOTTO

For 4

In spring, the stalls in the fruit and vegetable section of the Rialto Market are so laden with spoils of the new season that I sometimes think they might collapse. The grocers themselves shout, sing, grab, weigh, wrap, and sell at such a rate it sometimes appears that they have multiple arms, all working independently, like an octopus.

The vegetable that upstages all the others is the artichoke. There are thousands of them on a normal day in May, and they will most likely all be sold. You will see the famous purple artichokes from Sant'Erasmo, a few miles away in the lagoon, but there are also similar varieties from Liguria, Savona, and Tuscany. I tend to choose the smallest baby artichokes I can find. In Venice, I love the way the market traders always put a handful of flat parsley in the bag, unbidden. I have never worked out why this is (and it is only ever with artichokes), but it comes in very handy for this recipe.

6⅓ cups vegetable stock (see page 304)
extra virgin olive oil
20 baby artichokes, trimmed of their
*   stalks and hard outer leaves*
1 large white onion, finely chopped
1 clove of garlic, peeled and very
*   finely chopped*
a palmful of picked thyme leaves
flaky sea salt

a glass of white wine
1¾ cups Carnaroli rice
a small handful of basil leaves,
*   roughly torn*
a small handful of flat parsley leaves,
*   roughly chopped*
a large knob (about 2 tbsp) of butter
5¼ ounces Parmesan, grated
freshly ground black pepper

Heat the stock in a large saucepan and keep it simmering gently at the back of the stove.

In a separate large, heavy-bottomed pot for which you have a lid, heat a few glugs of olive oil and gently sauté the whole baby artichokes until they are starting to brown—about 5 minutes. Now add the chopped onion, garlic, and thyme with a good pinch of salt, and continue to gently sauté for an additional 5 minutes, until the onion is glossy and translucent but not browned. You may need to adjust the heat downward to prevent this. Add the glass of white wine, carefully stirring, and when it has almost all evaporated into that deliciously aromatic steam, add a large ladleful of stock. Cover the pot with the lid and very gently simmer for 10 minutes or so, until the artichokes are very tender.

Now, remove the artichokes and set them aside, add the rice to the pan, mix thoroughly with the onions, and add a ladleful of stock. When the liquid is almost all absorbed, add another ladleful of stock. Continue doing this, stirring gently, making sure the mixture never dries out but is not waterlogged either, for about 12 minutes.

Take four of the loveliest-looking cooked artichokes and carefully quarter them lengthwise. Roughly chop the remaining 16. Add the chopped artichokes to the risotto for the last 10 minutes or so of the cooking time, continuing to stir and adding more stock. When the rice is almost done (test a grain between your teeth—it should have a slight bite to it), add the basil, parsley, and the knob of butter. Stir thoroughly until the butter has melted and remove from the heat. Scatter in most of the Parmesan, fold a couple of times, then cover and rest for a minute.

Prepare four warmed plates and spoon the risotto carefully into the center of each. Evenly distribute the quartered artichokes and finish with a twist of black pepper, the remaining Parmesan, and a drizzle of olive oil.

VENETIAN RICE *and* PEAS

For 4

The morning of April 25 begins with mass at the Basilica. It is the beginning of a day of celebrations to honor the city's patron saint, St. Mark. The traditional gondola race, *the regata di traghetti*, starts very close to my apartment and I walk along the embankment, following it to the Doge's Palace. This represents a very rare trip into the historic center for me, but it is a special day in the Venetian calendar. It also coincides with the Festa del Bocolo (Festival of the Blooming Rose), during which gentlemen offer a single red rose to their wives, lovers, or girlfriends to commemorate the time a hapless soldier named Tancredi died on the battlefield, bled all over a nearby bloom, and insisted his friend Orlando take it back to his betrothed in Venice. Orlando did exactly that on April 25.

At lunchtime, I head to Alle Testiere, the tiny restaurant near Campo Santa Maria Formosa where Bruno Gavagnin, the chef, has prepared the traditional dish of St. Mark's Day, *risi e bisi*, aka rice and peas. It is a vibrant celebration of the first young fresh peas of the spring, but Bruno's recipe is earthy and powerful, the addition of pancetta and a rich stock making it feel like a meal in itself.

8½ cups chicken stock (see page 304)
5¼ ounces pancetta, cut into small cubes
extra virgin olive oil
1 large white onion, finely chopped
flaky sea salt
1⅔ cups Vialone Nano rice

a glass of dry vermouth
4½ pounds fresh peas in their pods, podded
    to yield 2¼ pounds peas
a large knob of butter
4¼ ounces Parmesan, grated
freshly ground black pepper

Heat the stock in a large pot and leave it at the back of the stove, simmering gently.

Place a frying pan over medium heat and add the cubed pancetta. You do not need to use oil—the pancetta will quickly release its own and happily cook in that for the 3 or 4 minutes required to take on a golden, crispy appearance. Remove from the heat and set aside.

Heat a few glugs of olive oil in a large, heavy-bottomed saucepan and gently sauté the chopped onion with a good pinch of salt. Stir, and after a few minutes, when the onion is beginning to turn glossy and translucent, add the rice. Make sure each grain is coated with oil, that the rice is starting to toast and is incorporated with the pearly chopped onions, then add the vermouth, stirring as it evaporates, which it will quite quickly. Without allowing the rice to dry out, add a ladleful of warm stock. Continue to cook gently, adding more stock as it is absorbed into the rice for the next 12 minutes. Add the peas and pancetta with another good ladleful of stock. Carry on stirring gently and adding more stock for the next 8 minutes, never letting the rice dry out but not flooding it either. Test a grain of rice between your teeth—it should have a soft resistance to your bite—and adjust the seasoning if necessary.

Add a final half-ladle of stock and stir. This is important, since *risi e bisi* should be looser and wetter than a regular risotto. Stir in the butter until it has melted, then fold through most of the Parmesan. Serve in large shallow bowls, with a scattering of the remaining Parmesan and a scant twist of black pepper.

SPAGHETTI *with* ONIONS

For 4

Everything starts with an onion. I love that simple ritual of peeling and chopping to create a small pile of pearly cubes. And when a recipe calls for a different means of preparation, as with this dish, the vegetable looks unfamiliar and somehow exotic. Ridiculous, I know, but it's like seeing an old friend in a different outfit.

This is a store-cupboard staple, a dish you should be able to make without going to the shops, assuming that every pantry has plenty of dried pasta, and that your kitchen, like mine, is never without onions. It is probably the dish made most frequently by my Venetian neighbors if they want a quick, no-fuss lunch, and it has become a favorite of mine, too.

6 medium white onions
2 tablespoons extra virgin olive oil
¾ cup plus 2 tablespoons chicken stock (see page 304)
1 pound dried spaghetti
a large knob of butter
flaky sea salt
freshly ground black pepper
a handful of flat parsley leaves, chopped
3½ ounces grated Parmesan

Peel the onions and, using a very sharp knife, carefully slice each one to create complete rings, around ¼ inch thick. Heat the olive oil in a large frying pan over low to medium heat. Add the sliced onions and slowly sauté for 12 to 15 minutes, stirring frequently to make sure they don't burn. They should take on a glossy, translucent appearance with a hint of golden brown here and there. Add the stock and cook for a further 10 minutes. If the stock bubbles too fiercely, reduce the heat.

Meanwhile, bring a large pot of salted water to a boil and cook the spaghetti according to the package instructions. When al dente, drain the pasta and add it to the frying pan. Mix well over a gentle heat, adding the butter, a generous pinch of salt and pepper, the parsley, and most of the Parmesan. Take off the heat, incorporate fully, and serve on warm plates with the remaining Parmesan scattered on top.

CRAB *and* CHILE LINGUINE

For 4

The common or garden crabs of the Venetian lagoon are upstaged every spring and autumn by the *moeche*—miraculous little molting crabs whose shells are soft for a tiny period of around nineteen hours. But the rest of the time, it's the spider crabs and larger Cromers that sit on the crushed ice slowly waving their claws and rotating their eyestalks. Their meat is delicious. Once cooked, they yield smoky, nutty, reddish-brown flesh from the body and fluffy, delicate white meat from the claws.

Your fishmonger, and most supermarket fish counters, will sell the meat already dressed and neatly packed, which makes this an easy (yet impressive and tasty) dish to prepare.

extra virgin olive oil
1 clove of garlic, finely chopped
1 red chile, deseeded and chopped
a small glass of white wine
5¼ ounces brown crabmeat
1 pound linguine
12 cherry tomatoes, halved
5¼ ounces white crabmeat
a large handful of flat parsley leaves, chopped
flaky sea salt
freshly ground black pepper
1 lemon

Heat a good glug of olive oil in a large frying pan over medium heat, and gently sauté the garlic and chile for a minute or two. Turn up the heat and pour in the white wine. When it starts to bubble fiercely, remove from the heat and add the brown crabmeat. Mix well into a paste.

Bring a large pot of salted water to a boil and add the linguine. Cook according to the package instructions minus 2 minutes. Retain a cupful of the cooking water, then drain the pasta. Add the linguine to the pan along with the tomatoes, return to a medium heat and mix well, stirring for a minute or two. Add the white crabmeat, the parsley, and a good pinch or two of salt. Stir well, using a little of the retained cooking water to loosen the sauce if necessary.

Serve on four warmed plates with a drizzle of olive oil, a twist of black pepper, and a squeeze of lemon.

SPAGHETTI *with* CLAMS, BOTTARGA, *and* WHIPPED PEAS

For 4

This dish was suggested to me by Francesco at Antiche Carampane, an excellent restaurant in what used to be Venice's red light district. This recipe is a delicious and fresh twist on the classic *spaghetti alle vongole*, and one I like to make when I've bought too many peas. Which is quite often.

extra virgin olive oil
2 large scallions, finely sliced
flaky sea salt
2 large handfuls of podded fresh peas
1 pound spaghetti
2¼ pounds Palourde clams, thoroughly
  scrubbed and cleaned

a glass of white wine
a handful of flat parsley leaves, roughly
  chopped
1¾ ounces bottarga
freshly ground black pepper

Heat a glug of olive oil in a frying pan and add the scallions with a pinch of salt. Gently sauté for about 5 minutes, until soft and translucent. Add the peas and continue to stir on a gentle heat for an additional 5 minutes. Now add 4 tablespoons of water and bring to a moderate bubble for 3 minutes. Remove from the heat and pour everything into a food processor or blender. Whiz for a minute while adding a very thin, slow stream of olive oil, no more than a tablespoon or so, until the mixture emulsifies slightly. Pour into a small jug and set aside.

Bring a large pot of salted water to a boil and add the spaghetti. Cook according to the package instructions minus 2 minutes.

Meanwhile, heat a large, high-sided sauté pan or heavy-bottomed saucepan over medium to high heat and add a good couple of glugs of olive oil. When the oil starts to crackle, throw in all the cleaned clams, add the glass of wine, and turn up the heat. Shake the pan vigorously all the while until the wine has mostly evaporated, about 3 to 4 minutes, and all the clams have opened. Discard any that have not.

Turn the heat down, remove about a third of the clams with a slotted spoon, and shell them, discarding the shells and returning the bivalves to the pan.

Retain a cup of the pasta cooking water and drain the almost-cooked spaghetti, putting it straight into the pan with the clams. Add the pea purée and the chopped parsley and stir vigorously to incorporate everything for a minute. It is important that the sauce created by the pea mixture and the clam juice coats every strand. Use a little of the retained pasta water to loosen the sauce but only if necessary; it should be nicely syrupy and glossy already.

Carefully distribute on four warmed plates, then, using a fine microplane grater, shave over generous amounts of bottarga. Add a twist of black pepper and serve.

SAUSAGE *and* EGG BUCATINI

For 4

I make this dish when I want pasta for breakfast. I also make it when my children ask for it. They like to help me cut the sausage meat out of the skins and roll it into little balls. I have to admit, I enjoy that part, too.

You could, of course, use any pasta shape you like with this sausage and egg sauce, but there is something particularly pleasing about the thickness of the bucatini and the fact that there's a tiny hole running all the way through it like a straw. My children have fun trying to suck air through the tubes. (If I'm honest, I might occasionally do that, too.)

4 excellent-quality spicy Italian sausages
flaky sea salt
1 pound dried bucatini
extra virgin olive oil
6 large egg yolks
5¼ ounces Parmesan, grated
freshly ground black pepper

Start by slicing the sausages lengthwise with a very sharp knife and pushing the sausage meat out into a bowl. Discard the skins. Add a pinch or two of salt and roll the meat into small balls, roughly 5 per sausage, 20 balls in total. Set them aside.

Bring a large pot of salted water to a boil and cook the bucatini according to the package instructions minus 1 minute.

Meanwhile, heat a couple of glugs of olive oil in a very large frying pan with deep sides, and sauté the sausage meat balls until they are golden brown on all sides. Turn the heat to very low.

Beat the egg yolks in a small mixing bowl and add most of the Parmesan, mixing together thoroughly.

Reserve a cup of the starchy pasta cooking water, drain the bucatini, add it to the pan with the sausage balls, and incorporate fully. Turn the stove off, pour in the yolk and cheese mixture, and turn over several times, adding several twists of black pepper. It is important that you allow the heat of the pasta to warm the egg mixture rather than the stove—this prevents the eggs turning to scramble. Loosen the sauce a little with the reserved pasta water if necessary.

Transfer equally to four warmed bowls, making sure all the eggy, cheesy sauce is used, and finish with the remaining Parmesan and a final good twist of black pepper.

SMALL GNOCCHI *with* BABY SQUID *and* CINNAMON

For 4

It is often surprising to a Venice novice how frequently cinnamon appears in the cooking of the region, although it is not such an anomaly when you consider the Serene Republic's history as an east/west trading post and Venice's importance as the pivotal port on the historic spice route.

Bruno Gavagnin, the co-proprietor and chef at Alle Testiere, one of the city's most consistently excellent restaurants, cooks a very similar dish but somehow manages to find the tiniest squid, barely larger than plump spiders. If I can't locate the babies at the market, I will sometimes separate the tentacle section and then cut the bodies in two.

4 medium-large floury potatoes
   (about 1¾ pounds)
1½ cups "00" flour, plus more for dusting
3 large egg yolks, whisked
fine salt
extra virgin olive oil
1 clove of garlic, crushed
14 ounces very small (baby) squid, cleaned

flaky sea salt
ground cinnamon
freshly ground black pepper
a small glass of white wine
a small handful of flat parsley leaves,
   chopped
a large knob of butter

Bring a large pot of salted water to a boil and cook the potatoes, whole, for about 20 minutes, until a skewer can be pushed easily into the center without too much resistance. Drain them, and when they are cool enough to handle, peel and set aside.

Dust a large wooden chopping board or work surface with flour. Push the potatoes through a ricer or sieve onto the floured surface and dust with a little more flour. Create a well in the middle and drop in the egg yolks and a good pinch of fine salt. Using floured hands, and adding more flour as required, knead and work the mixture until you have a smooth, even dough.

With a very sharp knife, cut the dough into about 6 even pieces and, using floured hands, roll each piece into a long, thin log, around ½ inch thick. Cut the logs into ¾ inch sections. These little rectangles are your gnocchi. Dust with flour and transfer to floured trays, making sure the gnocchi do not touch each other. Leave in a cool place.

Heat 3 tablespoons of olive oil in a very large saucepan over a medium heat. Gently sauté the garlic, then add the baby squid, a pinch of flaky salt, a pinch of cinnamon and a good twist of black pepper. Cook the squid for about 2 to 3 minutes, until they start to color, then add the white wine. Stir and continue to sauté for a further 3 minutes, then remove from the heat.

Meanwhile, bring a large pot of salted water to a boil and carefully add the gnocchi. When they rise to the surface they are done, so remove with a slotted spoon and add to the pan of squid. You will need to do this in two or three batches.

When all the gnocchi are transferred, add the chopped parsley and the butter and cook over high heat for 30 seconds, adding a splash of the gnocchi cooking water. Divide equally between four warmed bowls and serve immediately, with a final scant sprinkling of cinnamon.

GRILLED SPRING VEGETABLE PIZZA

For 1

This is such a fresh and delightful pizza. It feels hearty and comforting, like all good pizzas should, but also faintly virtuous and healthy with all those lovely spring vegetables. I like making it for vegetarian friends, and you can even opt for rennet-free mozzarella if you want to go the whole nine yards.

I usually order it when I go to Dai Tosi, a charming pizzeria just around the corner from my apartment. It is owned and run by Jackie and Paulo (she's British, he's Venetian) and it is packed to the rafters most evenings. On warm nights, the tables spill out into the street and it feels like you're at the best party in Venice. It may sound like an anomaly (and, yes, I know pizza originates in Naples), but this is as close to a "Venetian" pizza as you can get without actually visiting Dai Tosi yourself.

1 small zucchini
½ a small eggplant
½ a red or orange pepper, deseeded
2 green or white asparagus spears
extra virgin olive oil
flaky sea salt

a satsuma-size ball of pizza dough
*   (see page 301)*
2 tablespoons tomato sauce (see page 300)
a very large handful of grated mozzarella
freshly ground black pepper

Slice the zucchini and eggplant lengthwise into ⅛-inch thick strips. Cut the pith from the pepper and slice into strips. Remove the woody stalks and slice the asparagus lengthwise. Lightly coat all in a little olive oil.

Set a grill pan over high heat until it starts to smoke and grill all the sliced vegetables, with a few good pinches of salt, until softened and showing strong, dark grill lines. Remove and set aside on paper towels.

Flatten and stretch the dough on a floured surface until it is a rough disk of around 9 inches or so. Don't roll it too neatly. If your disks go a bit wonky, even better. I love those uneven shapes. Leave the edges a little thicker. Place it on a greased baking sheet.

Using a tablespoon, spread the tomato sauce evenly over the dough base, stopping about ½ inch from the edge. Preheat the oven as high as it will go.

Distribute the grated mozzarella onto the tomato base and scatter the grilled vegetables evenly. Add a pinch of salt, a twist of black pepper, and drizzle with a little olive oil. Place your pizza in the hot oven and keep a very close eye on it. It will take anywhere from 5 to 8 minutes to bake, depending on your oven. You should see a little browning at the edges and the occasional blister, but you mustn't let it burn.

RED ONION PIZZA

For 1

Often the simplest toppings work best on a pizza. Aficionados will tell you the only true pizza is the Marinara (see page 118), breathtakingly simple with just tomato sauce, garlic, and dried oregano (no mozzarella), and, if those same experts are feeling generous, they'll concede the Margherita, too, that classic buffalo mozzarella, tomato, and basil combination. In fact, the most famous pizzeria in Naples, da Michele, offers these two options and nothing else.

This pizza works so well because, when roasted, red onion is a sweet, intense, softly textured revelation. The transformation is often quite surprising to the uninitiated. Be sure to use an entire red onion per pizza and don't skimp on the mozzarella.

a satsuma-size ball of pizza dough
  (see page 301)
extra virgin olive oil
2 tablespoons tomato sauce (see page 300)

1 large red onion, peeled
a very large handful of grated mozzarella
freshly ground black pepper
flaky sea salt

Flatten and stretch the dough on a floured surface until it is a rough disk of around 9 inches or so. Try to resist the temptation to roll it too neatly. Leave the edges a bit thicker. Place it on a lightly oiled baking sheet.

Using the back of a tablespoon, spread the tomato sauce evenly over the dough base, stopping about ½ inch from the edge. Preheat the oven as high as it will go.

Using a sharp knife, slice the onion thinly into disks and separate the rings with your hands. Scatter the grated mozzarella over the pizza base, add a twist of pepper, and a pinch or two of salt, and evenly distribute the red onion over the top. Drizzle with a little olive oil and place the baking sheet directly on the top shelf of the oven, closing the door quickly. Bake for around 5 minutes but keep an eye on it and remove when the edges are starting to darken and the cheese is bubbling a little.

Remove and scatter over the Parmesan, with a scant drizzle of olive oil, a pinch of salt, and a twist of black pepper.

FRITTATA *with* PRAWNS *and* DILL

For 4

One of my neighbors on the Corte de Ca' Sarasina has a daily routine that goes something like this. She pats the heads of her children as they skip to school, takes her wheelie basket to the market, comes back, bakes a cake, takes a bucket of hot, soapy water onto the street and washes her step, pops back in for a coffee, makes lunch, eats it, does the washing, hangs it out to dry, cooks the evening meal, has a nap, and then the kids come home. She normally greets them on the newly gleaming step holding out a snack for them to eat, and often it's a thick wedge of cold frittata.

Frittata is rarely eaten hot, and it is only by leaving it to cool or eating it cold from the fridge the following day that you get to appreciate the gently firm but yielding texture that is such an important aspect of the dish. This one with prawns and dill is perfect for lunch on a sunny day or as a snack for hungry schoolchildren.

extra virgin olive oil
1 small onion, peeled and sliced
4¼ ounces small cooked prawns, peeled
flaky sea salt
whole milk
4 medium eggs, beaten
a small handful of dill
freshly ground black pepper

Heat a glug of olive oil in a smallish nonstick frying pan (all-metal, no plastic handles for this recipe please) over low heat. Sauté the onion for 8 minutes, until soft and translucent. Add the prawns with a good pinch of salt and stir a few times to coat them in the oil and incorporate with the onions. Put a splash of milk in with the beaten eggs and pour everything into the pan. Stir in the dill. Preheat the broiler.

Leave the pan over low heat for about 10 minutes, until the frittata is mostly solid, but the top surface is still a little liquid and pale. Put the pan under the broiler until the top is golden brown. Remove carefully using oven gloves—the handle may be very hot—and allow to cool. Turn onto a plate and serve warm, in quarters, with a twist of black pepper and a crunchy salad, or put it into the fridge to serve cold the next day with a pinch of flaky sea salt.

JOHN DORY *with* ASPARAGUS *and* BASIL

For 4

On a gloriously bright day in April, I'd returned from the market with a bunch of handsome local asparagus, some small John Dory fillets, and a couple of limes.

I knew in my head the flavors I craved, but my first instinct to fry the John Dory was wrong. So the compromise was that the beautiful white fillets retain their elegance by being gently poached in the fish stock. The tang and aromatics from the lime and basil do the donkey work and leave the John Dory and asparagus to be themselves. Sometimes you have to be a diplomat in the kitchen.

16 slender asparagus spears
about 10 green or pink peppercorns
extra virgin olive oil
4 John Dory fillets, small
flaky sea salt

⅔ cup fish stock (see page 305)
2 limes, one juiced, one quartered
a large handful of basil leaves, shredded
a large knob of butter

Prepare the asparagus by cutting off the woody ends and, using a speed peeler, tapering the base of each stalk to reveal the pale green flesh. Bring a pan of salted water to a boil and blanch the asparagus for 3 to 4 minutes, then drain, rinse in cold water, and set aside.

Put the green peppercorns into a mortar and pestle and pound them a few times. Set aside.

In a large sauté pan for which you have a lid, gently heat 2 tablespoons of olive oil. Put the John Dory fillets into the pan with a good pinch of salt. When the fish starts to hiss, add the fish stock and the lime juice and cover with the lid. Cook the fish in this way for about 3 minutes. Remove the lid, turn the fillets over, and add the blanched asparagus and half the basil. Spoon the stock and lime juice mixture over the fish, replace the lid, and poach for an additional 2 minutes.

Remove the fillets to warmed plates and equally distribute the asparagus spears, leaving the pan on the stove. Turn the heat up to high, add the butter and the remaining shredded basil, and reduce the sauce to a syrupy consistency, about 2 minutes.

Pour the sauce over the John Dory, scatter the peppercorns over evenly, and serve with a wedge of lime.

MACKEREL CAPONATA

For 4

I was inspired to make this after watching my friend Francesco Zorzetto serve little pots of mackerel and tomato in his charming wine bar La Cantina, on Strada Nova in Cannaregio. He used mixed yellow and red tomatoes to great effect, and I suggest you do the same. It lends the dish a particularly cheerful demeanor.

Caponata is, strictly speaking, a Sicilian dish, the region's answer to ratatouille. I'm aware that I'm stretching the definition of that southern favorite here, since my version contains neither eggplant nor capers, but the principle is the same and its heart is in the right place. You can, of course, use any Italian olive, but if you can find the tiny Taggiasca variety from Liguria, all the better. They have just the right amount of bitterness.

extra virgin olive oil
a small bunch of scallions, finely sliced
flaky sea salt
1 clove of garlic, peeled and very finely sliced
1 yellow pepper, deseeded, cored, and sliced
red wine vinegar
24 small, sweet tomatoes
24 Taggiasca olives

2 tablespoons tomato purée
4 mackerel fillets, medium
freshly ground black pepper
a handful of flat parsley leaves,
*   roughly chopped*
a small handful of basil leaves

Heat 2 tablespoons of olive oil in a large, heavy-bottomed saucepan and gently sauté the scallions with a good pinch of salt for about 5 minutes, until soft and glossy, but not browned at all. Add the garlic, the sliced pepper, a splash of red wine vinegar, and the tomatoes.

Turn up the heat just a fraction and continue to carefully stir and fry, making sure nothing burns, until the tomatoes start to crinkle or split. At this point, add the olives, the tomato purée, and about ⅔ cup of water and stir. Bring to a very brief boil, then turn right down to a very low simmer for around 15 minutes.

Meanwhile, warm a good glug of olive oil in a frying pan or grill pan over medium heat. Sprinkle the mackerel fillets with a little salt and a twist of black pepper. Lay them skin side down in the pan for a minute and a half, then flip them over for a minute or so on the other side, too.

When there are only 3 minutes left of the caponata cooking time, carefully transfer the fillets to the saucepan. Submerge them a little, being careful not to squash them, and spoon over the sauce. Test and adjust the seasoning. Turn up the heat for the last minute, and add the chopped parsley and basil. Serve on warmed plates, making sure the mackerel fillets are skin side up, and spooning over every last drop of the sauce.

VIGNOLE

For 4

My favorite way to start making this spring classic is to put a small table and a chair on the balcony overlooking the washing lines along the street, and sit in the sun to pod all the peas and shell all the broad beans. I always try very hard not to eat all the peas raw, straight from the pod, and will often buy more than I need to compensate for my lack of willpower.

If you see baby spring leeks at the greengrocer, buy a couple of those, too, wash and slice them, and put them into the pan with the onion. This is delicious on a hot day served at room temperature, perhaps as an accompaniment to a simply grilled fillet of sea bream.

*8 baby artichokes, trimmed of hard outer
    leaves and woody stalk*
*2¼ pounds fresh baby broad (fava) beans
    in their pods, podded to yield 9 ounces
    beans*
10½ ounces chard, chopped roughly
extra virgin olive oil
a large knob of good butter
1 large white onion, peeled and

finely chopped
1½ cups chicken stock (see page 304)
*2¼ pounds fresh peas in their pods, podded
    to yield 1 pound 1 ounce peas*
6 thick slices of prosciutto, cut into ribbons
*a large handful of mint leaves, picked
    and washed*
flaky sea salt
freshly ground black pepper

Bring a large pot of salted water to a boil and add the artichokes. Blanch for 10 minutes until just tender—you can test this by pushing a knife into the heart; it should offer little resistance—and drain. When they have cooled, peel off and discard any hard outer leaves that remain. Trim and peel the stem if still woody, until you reach the tender flesh. Cut each artichoke into quarters and set aside.

In a fresh pan of salted boiling water, blanch the broad beans for 2 minutes and remove with a slotted spoon. Now add the chard for a minute or two until it starts to wilt. Drain and set aside.

Heat 2 tablespoons of olive oil with the butter in a very large saucepan. Soften the onion for 10 minutes, then add the stock and the peas. Bring to a boil very briefly, then add the prosciutto and reduce to a simmer. Let it all bubble gently for 10 minutes. Add the artichokes, broad beans, and chard and simmer again for 8 to 10 minutes. Roughly chop the mint and stir in with a good pinch of salt and a twist of pepper.

Taste and adjust the seasoning if necessary, then add a good glug of olive oil, stir a few times, and serve on warmed plates with a hunk of crusty bread.

BRAISED PEAS *with* BASIL

For 4, as a starter

This is a very typical Venetian preparation for young, tender peas and one that is perfect to start off a meal and get the taste buds tingling. On April 25 peas are always used to make a classic risi e bisi (see page 46) for the feast day of St. Mark, but for the rest of the season this is one of my favorites—a refreshing and vibrant appetizer. Peas tend to get paired with mint, habitually, but they work beautifully with basil, lending them a particularly fragrant and sunny disposition.

8 large scallions or 16 slender ones
1 large celery stalk
extra virgin olive oil
1 clove of garlic, peeled and very thinly sliced
2¼ pounds fresh peas in their pods, podded to yield 1 pound 1 ounce peas
flaky sea salt
freshly ground black pepper
1¼ cups vegetable stock (see page 304)
2 large handfuls of basil leaves, roughly torn

Thinly slice the scallions on the diagonal. Use the whole length, including the green shank, but not the root fronds. Cut the celery in half lengthwise, then slice very thinly.

Pour a good few glugs of olive oil into a large frying pan and place over medium heat. Gently sauté the sliced onion and celery for about 5 minutes, until nicely soft and glossy but not browned. Add the garlic and stir slowly for a minute, also making sure it does not take on any color—you may need to turn the heat down a little.

Now add nearly all the peas with a good pinch of salt and a twist of black pepper. (Retain a handful of the smallest peas.) Stir, then pour in enough stock to only just cover all the greenery. Turn the heat up just enough to get the stock gently bubbling and cook for about 6 to 8 minutes, until the sauce has reduced and the dish has taken on a slightly syrupy consistency but the peas are still green and round—you must not let them wrinkle.

Remove the pan from the heat, stir in the basil and the remaining small raw peas, test and adjust the seasoning if necessary, then leave to rest for a minute or two. Serve warm.

ESPRESSO MARTINI

For 1

The late Dick Bradsell, one of the most influential bartenders of the last fifty years, invented this cocktail, and I'm afraid he would turn in his grave to hear it referred to as an Espresso Martini. Dick always called it the Vodka Espresso. It's a remarkably successful combination of bitterness and sweetness and it's a perfect way to end a long evening of eating and drinking well. In Venice, the best place to drink these is at the rooftop bar of the Commedia Hotel near Rialto Bridge. The inestimable Giovanni d'Este introduced me to this infrequent sin after a few drinks at his tiny *osteria*, I Rusteghi. It is not something I do often but it feels like a special treat when I do.

3 tablespoons vodka
1½ tablespoons Tia Maria or Kahlúa
1½ tablespoons espresso

a dash of simple syrup
3 coffee beans, to garnish

Fill a cocktail shaker with ice and add the four liquid ingredients. (Good, strong coffee from a stovetop Bialetti moka coffeemaker will suffice if you don't have access to an espresso machine, but there's no reason you can't get takeout espresso earlier in the day and leave it on the side.)

Shake enthusiastically for 15 to 20 seconds, then, using a clean tea strainer or a fine sieve, strain into a chilled, classic 5-ounce Martini glass. The drink will have a satisfying foam on to which you should place the three coffee beans.

PINZA

Makes 12 big squares

Like many Venetian puddings, *pinza* is often made at Easter but it first appears much earlier, on Twelfth Night. It is a classic domestic dessert, something that is so traditional in the homes of the region that I have rarely seen it produced commercially. It's also something of a family activity to make; even clumsy *pinzas* crafted by tiny hands turn out rather well (some might say for the better).

It is always cut into satisfying, solid squares, by the way. Don't try getting fancy with thin slices, it just wouldn't be right.

4 tablespoons raisins	*1⅔ cups whole milk*
2 tablespoons dried figs, chopped	*2½ cups polenta flour*
2 tablespoons pine nuts	*1½ cups "00" flour*
the zest of 2 oranges	*⅔ cup superfine sugar*
2 teaspoons fennel seeds	*2 packets of dried yeast (⅔ cup)*
⅓ cup grappa	*1¾ sticks salted butter*

Soak the raisins, chopped figs, pine nuts, orange zest, and fennel seeds in the grappa for about half an hour. Fill a kettle with water and boil.

Bring the milk to a boil in a very large saucepan and immediately mix both the flours into the hot milk, stirring with a wooden spoon. Add the sugar, the dried yeast, a good splash or two of the boiled water and all the butter, and stir to create a dough with the consistency of porridge. Add a little more boiled water if necessary. Stir in the soaked ingredients and a splash of the grappa. Turn off the heat and continue to mix for a few minutes. Pour the mixture onto a large, deep baking tray lined with parchment paper. Cover loosely with a damp cloth and leave in a warm place for 2 hours.

Preheat the oven to 350°F/180°C. Place the tray on the middle shelf and bake for about 45 minutes, until golden brown. Leave to cool slightly for 15 minutes, then cut into 3-inch squares and serve warm with coffee or a sticky, sweet wine. Moscato is ideal.

ZALETI

Makes about 36

My friend Martina Gerotto invited me to a picnic on the island of Torcello. She and her husband have a garden there where they grow a few vegetables and keep chickens. It is only accessible by private boat and yet there were over a hundred people one beautiful spring Sunday, all enjoying the sunshine, some live music, a little dancing, and a huge feast made up of a variety of dishes, all of which had been brought by the individuals attending. Martina's sister Anna contributed a large tray of these curious yellow cookies, which were delicious, particularly with a glass of Vin Santo.

The name, incidentally, comes from the Venetian dialect word for yellow—*zalo*—and I have seen them made with pine nuts, but I like Anna's version with the grappa-soaked raisins.

3 ½ ounces raisins
¼ cup grappa
1 cup superfine sugar
4 medium eggs
2 cups cornstarch
2 cups plain flour

2 teaspoons fine salt
1 teaspoon vanilla extract
the zest of 1 lemon
1 ¾ sticks butter, softened
a little milk
confectioners' sugar, to dust

Soak the raisins in the grappa for about an hour. Drain them before using.

Put the sugar and eggs into a large bowl and beat them together until pale and fluffy. Set aside.

Mix the cornstarch and flour together and add the salt, vanilla extract, and lemon zest. Now add the sugar and egg mixture, along with the softened butter and drained raisins, and knead well into a dough, adding a little milk if too dry or a little more flour if too wet.

Preheat the oven to 350°F / 180°C and roll the dough into a fat rope around ¾ inch thick. Cut at an angle to create 2-inch-long diamond shapes and lay them on a buttered baking sheet.

Bake for around 12 to 15 minutes, until golden brown, then remove from the oven and sprinkle with confectioners' sugar. Allow to cool, and serve with sweet wine.

TOBLERONE ZABAIONE

For 6

It is a cliché, I know, but so often, when family and friends come to visit me in Venice, they will bring me a bar of Toblerone. It is so ubiquitous at the airport and seems to be the last-minute gift of choice for the desperate person, the confectionery equivalent of flowers from the petrol station.

They tend to sit on the side, untouched, until I can find a child to eat them. If you can't locate a young person, this recipe makes excellent use of the classic triangular Swiss chocolate nougat bar and, furthermore, I have corrected it in the traditional Venetian manner by adding booze. It works particularly well with dark Toblerone.

6 large egg yolks
⅔ cup superfine sugar
⅔ cup Marsala
1 large dark Toblerone bar (12.7 ounces)
¼ cup Vecchia Romagna (or other brandy)
½ cup double cream

Take a heatproof Pyrex bowl that will fit neatly inside a saucepan without touching the bottom. Put the egg yolks and sugar into the bowl. Whisk for 3 minutes or so, until you have a smooth, silky foam. Whisk in the Marsala.

Now, half-fill the saucepan with water and bring to a boil. Place the bowl over the saucepan so that it fits snugly (but does not touch the water) and beat the mixture until it starts to thicken. Divide the *zabaione* equally between six pretty glasses, allow to cool, then refrigerate for 30 minutes.

Meanwhile, using a clean heatproof Pyrex dish, break up the Toblerone bar and melt using the same bain-marie method as above. When the chocolate has melted, stir in the brandy and the cream until smooth.

Remove the glasses from the fridge, pour the melted Toblerone over the *zabaione*, and serve immediately.

SMALL WILD STRAWBERRIES
with TARRAGON

For 4

Strawberries are one of those sunshine ingredients. In Venice, they start to appear in the spring and my favorite variety is the tiny *fragolini di bosco* (small strawberries of the forest) that I can usually buy at the Rialto fruit and vegetable market from late April or early May. I happen to think that it is rather foolish to do anything to them other than wash, dry, and eat them. I did consider simply writing the following recipe:

Buy the strawberries

Wash the strawberries

Eat the strawberries

but I was concerned this might represent a degree of chutzpah that would make even me flinch. Nonetheless, this is a very simple preparation and it introduces two flavors that go exceptionally well with the fruit: balsamic vinegar and tarragon. The former enhances their natural sweetness and the latter brings a hint of licorice that is transformative. Please use exceptionally good balsamic vinegar.

1¾ pounds fragolini di bosco or small wild strawberries
a small handful of tarragon leaves, finely shredded
1 tablespoon superfine sugar
1 tablespoon excellent balsamic vinegar

Wash and thoroughly dry the strawberries. Any excess water will dilute the flavors of this dish. Remove the stalks carefully with your index finger and thumb. With a little practice you should be able to pull out the little core along with the stalk. Cut each strawberry in half lengthwise and place in a large mixing bowl.

Add the shredded tarragon, the superfine sugar, and the balsamic vinegar and gently turn over several times with your hand. Please be delicate.

Divide equally among four wide bowls. I really don't think you need anything else (except, perhaps, a scoop of very good vanilla ice cream).

TOMATO AND OREGANO BRUSCHETTA • SMOKED MACKEREL PANZANELLA • PEA, BROAD BEAN, AND STRACCHINO BRUSCHETTA • MINESTRA ALLA GENOVESE • LOBSTER AND FENNEL SOUP • MUSSEL SOUP • FENNEL, MINT, AND ORANGE SALAD • FRESH SPAGHETTI WITH RAW PEAS, YOUNG PECORINO, AND MINT • SPAGHETTI CASSOPIPA • BUCATINI WITH SARDINES AND SCALLIONS • SPAGHETTINI WITH OVEN-DRIED TOMATOES, CHILE, AND GARLIC • PEA, CHANTERELLE, AND ASPARAGUS RISOTTO • LINGUINE WITH CLAMS AND RAPINI • AGED PARMESAN RISOTTO • ZUCCHINI, MINT, AND GOAT'S CHEESE RISOTTO • SPINACH AND RICOTTA MALFATTI • PIZZA MARINARA • FRIED PIZZETTA MARGHERITA • BUTTER-FRIED JOHN DORY • SWEET AND SOUR SLIP SOLES • RAZOR CLAMS • SWORDFISH PUTTANESCA • SEA BASS IN CRAZY WATER • MASHED BROAD BEANS WITH GREMOLATA • AMALFI LEMONADE • MY GIN MARTINI • BELLINI SORBET • ALMOND CAKE • NECTARINES WITH WALNUTS, ROSEMARY, AND GORGONZOLA • CHOCOLATE, HAZELNUT, AND NOUGAT SEMIFREDDO

SUMMER

"It is the city of mirrors, the city of mirages, at once solid and liquid, at once air and stone." *Erica Jong*

✳

I have never asked for directions in Venice. This is not because I carry a map, or that I have a photographic memory (although now, after more than thirty years, I know my way around reasonably well), nor is it because I am too proud. It is because I have always enjoyed getting lost. One of the most remarkable attributes of the city's topography is that you can be struggling against the tide of a huge crowd one minute on a busy thoroughfare and yet, after just two or three turns, find yourself in a silent, deserted courtyard, bedsheets flapping from a washing line and a stray cat rubbing against your leg. I once made a wrong turn on a fresh, early summer's morning only to chance upon a small *campo* filled with around eighty tiny children, all dressed in little tunics and aprons, playing ball, shouting, singing, skipping and laughing, chaperoned by two nuns in full habit and wimple.

Getting lost in Venice is a rite of passage. It is also the best way to discover the city. Where is the adventure in always going exactly where you need to be? If you know where you've left, and you know where you're going, there's little in between but the route, which you probably know too. Much better to occasionally go off-piste and surprise yourself. There is little point in asking a Venetian for directions anyway. They always wave a hand vaguely in front of them and say *sempre dritto*—"straight ahead." I suppose the implication is that you'll get where you need to eventually.

The street signs are another matter entirely. With the exception of the *niziolèti* (traditional Venetian signs with black stenciled lettering on a large white rectangle) that tell you where you are, the directional ones seem to be designed to deliberately confuse. Often you will come across an official sign for, say, San Marco, where the arrow points both left and right simultaneously (Schrödinger's directions?). At other times, the arrow will have been crossed out and a new one graffitied in its place pointing somewhere else entirely.

In summer, the rule book is torn up completely, however. Venice becomes more challenging than in any other season. The streets are impassable because of the sheer quantity of tourists, and getting lost is no longer an option because it is impossible to move. In addition, the heat is stifling and the air is heavy and thick with humidity and mosquitoes. Most Venetians shut up shop and leave for the entire month of August, escaping to holiday homes on the mainland or decamping to airier parts of the world.

The smaller islands of the lagoon offer some relief. Those sandy beaches on the ocean side of the Lido are popular in the summer. Burano, although overrun with tourists between 10 a.m. and 4 p.m. every day, is an oasis of calm and civility in the evening. Mazzorbo, with its skew-whiff bell tower and beautiful vineyards, is generally under-visited and peaceful. And Torcello, once the center of the Republic, now appears like a dream, a memory of its former glory. Some of my Venetian friends have private gardens on Torcello so that on hot days they can jump into their boats and spend the afternoon in peace beneath the shade of their fruit trees.

After the festival of Redentore in July, when the Giudecca Canal is lit up by the most spectacular firework display and Venetians give thanks to the Holy Redeemer for being delivered from the catastrophic plague of 1576, I tend to avoid the historic center of the city entirely and travel to the outer islands, eat modestly, visit friends, or take a cycle ride along the Lido and swim in the Adriatic off the beaches of Pellestrina. It is at this time of the year that I seek out the simple. What could be better on a hot day than setting up a small table and chair on the balcony, cutting a few triangles of cheese, laying out a couple of slices of good Parma ham with some halved, salted cherry tomatoes, and enjoying this simple spread with a glass of cold Soave, a crusty bread, and some olive oil? Might that just be the perfect lunch?

I make no apologies for the fact that this chapter relies less on traditional Venetian cooking and represents a more spontaneous response to the markets, and to the ingredients that summer has to offer. I could happily spend the full length of the season without once turning on the stove or lighting the oven. Raw food, salads, assembly rather than cooking tend to be the order of the day.

One day in June, I suppose just after the schools had broken up for the summer, I was told that the following afternoon there would be some sort of open-air feast. It seemed impromptu but immediately the atmosphere changed and all activity on the street was focused on the event. I prepared a few salads and sealed them in large Tupperware boxes. I made some store-cupboard crostini, too (mashed anchovy and chickpeas on toast) and began to get a little curious about the next day's street party.

As it transpired, it was more of a casual picnic than a formal outdoor feast, but it brought the community together and I got to try some of the wonderful home cooking of my neighbors: a large poached salmon with summer berries, tiny fried baby squid, garlicky *bovoletti* snails, plenty of salami and cheese, and a large tray of marinated slip soles *in saor* by which I loitered for a little too long. (My recipe is on page 122.)

My favorite time of the day in the summer months is early morning. In July, the sun rises at around 5:30 a.m. but the sky starts to get light a good forty minutes beforehand. The first sound is the swifts, screeching in the skies above as they swirl and swoop to catch their breakfast of flying insects. After opening all the windows and the balcony doors, the symphony of the city floods the apartment: vaporetti engines, church bells, birds, seagulls, delivery men, the garbage collection, the postman, neighbors talking. It never gets routine, never ceases to thrill, always sounds exciting, and it helps me start every day with a spring in my step. It also presents me with an appetite and a question: What's for lunch?

TOMATO *and* OREGANO BRUSCHETTA

For 4

Bad tomatoes upset me. It really isn't worth bothering with them unless they are first-rate. And at the wrong time of the year (October through to April) you will only ever get imports from the wrong hemisphere or fruits that are grown hydroponically in a laboratory environment.

Italian home cooks will use only excellent tomatoes that are ripe and full of flavor. Please adopt this philosophy when shopping for this simple iteration of a much-loved bruschetta. I have substituted oregano leaves for the usual basil—it lends an earthiness that suits the slightly thicker slices of bread, even better if charred on a grill.

1⅓ pounds excellent ripe tomatoes
flaky sea salt
a handful of plump oregano leaves, stalks removed
extra virgin olive oil
4 slices of Pugliese or sourdough, 1½ inches thick
1 clove of garlic, peeled
freshly ground black pepper

Give yourself plenty of space with a large chopping board and a very sharp or serrated knife. First making sure the tomatoes are at room temperature, carefully cut them into pieces around the size of small dice. Shape isn't important, but creating as much surface area as possible is key. I like to discard the stalky bits from the crown but keep the seeds and juice, of which there should be plenty. Transfer the chopped tomatoes into a large bowl and scatter over a generous amount of salt. Leave to stand for 10 minutes.

Tear any large leaves of oregano in half and add to the tomatoes with a good glug of olive oil. Stir once or twice. Keep the small oregano leaves intact and set aside.

Grill the slices of bread until they are lightly charred but still have a little spring when pressed with a finger. (If you have a charcoal grill, even better. A few minutes over hot coals does wonders for the flavor.) Rub the garlic clove over one side of each slice. Taste the tomatoes and add more salt if necessary, then spoon generously over the grilled bread. Scatter over the remaining small oregano leaves evenly with a twist of black pepper and a drizzle of olive oil, then cut the slices in half and serve.

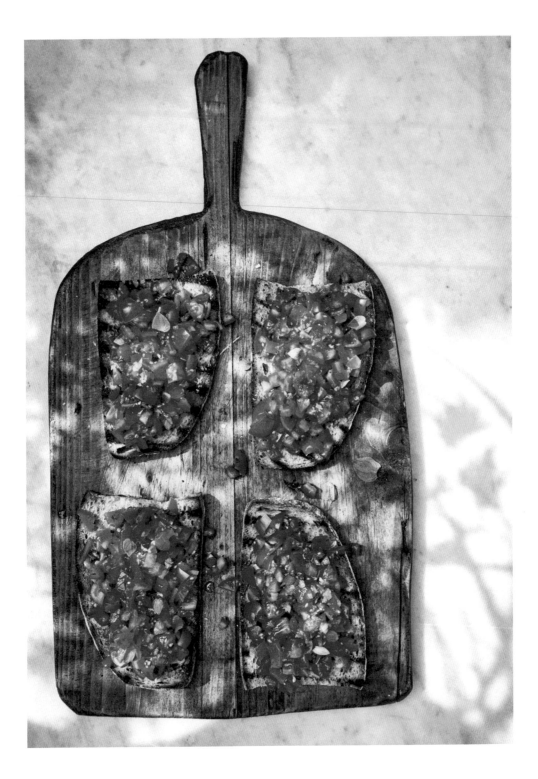

SMOKED MACKEREL PANZANELLA

For 4

The small supermarket on Via Garibaldi is always busy and local custom dictates that you leave your wheeled shopping basket outside, creating a funny little parking lot.

I sometimes like to explore the well-stocked shelves and was intrigued one day to see vacuum-packed smoked mackerel fillets in the chiller cabinet. Back home, with a significant number of tomatoes to use up, and some day-old country bread, the Tuscan peasant staple *panzanella* sprang to mind. Flaking the smoked mackerel through it made a fantastically tangy salad, and this is a dish I have made several times since with a few tweaks. It's a perfect quick lunch and a summer family favorite.

5¼ ounces sourdough bread
a large knob of butter
2 smoked mackerel fillets, unskinned
20 excellent ripe tomatoes, various sizes
flaky sea salt
freshly ground black pepper
extra virgin olive oil
red wine vinegar
a handful of basil leaves

First, tear the sourdough into small, rough, bite-size pieces. Put a frying pan over medium heat and melt the butter. Gently sauté the bread pieces until fully coated, golden, and crispy. Set aside.

Next, place the smoked mackerel fillets on a chopping board and, using two forks, pull the flesh in opposite directions to create stringy strands. Set aside.

On a clean chopping board, cut the tomatoes into bite-size pieces, discarding any stalky cores, and place them in a very large mixing bowl. Crunch over a few pinches of flaky salt and a twist or two of black pepper. Add a few glugs of olive oil and about a tablespoon of red wine vinegar. Turn the tomatoes over a few times with your hand. The juice from the tomatoes will start to combine with the oil and vinegar. Add the mackerel, sourdough, and basil and turn over once or twice.

Let stand for 10 minutes, then turn everything over one last time and divide equally into four large bowls, making sure you pour over the residual juices.

PEA, BROAD BEAN, *and* STRACCHINO BRUSCHETTA

For 4

At the start of summer, broad beans tend to be small and delicate and I will sometimes eat them briefly boiled and salted with a little olive oil and lemon. They look and taste delicious in their little pale membranes. When they start to get large in high summer, however, the individual beans must be blanched and popped out of their skins. This reveals them in their stunning vibrant greenness and makes them a lot more versatile. Here, crushed together with raw peas, they are thrilling and I can't think of a taste that is as fresh and as summery. Try to use freshly picked mint if you are fortunate enough to have it growing in your garden or on your windowsill; it releases a little minty oil as it is chopped. Stracchino is a mild, spreadable cow's milk cheese from Lombardy. If your Italian deli doesn't stock it, you could use Bel Paese instead.

1 ¾ pounds fresh broad (fava) beans in their pods, podded to yield ½ pound beans
14 ounces fresh peas in their pods, podded to yield 7 ounces peas
flaky sea salt
the juice and zest of ½ a lemon

a large handful of mint leaves, well chopped
extra virgin olive oil
4 slices of soda bread, ¾ inch thick
2 cloves of garlic, peeled
7 ounces stracchino cheese
freshly ground black pepper

Bring a saucepan of salted water to a boil and cook the broad beans for 3 minutes. Drain, rinse in cold water, and when cool enough to handle, pinch the beans out of their little membranes and discard the skins.

Put the cooked, skinned broad beans and raw peas into a large mortar and pestle with a good pinch of sea salt and crush well. You will need to do this in batches. Transfer the mixture to a larger bowl and mix in the lemon juice and chopped mint. Add a glug of olive oil, stir, taste and adjust the seasoning if necessary.

Grill or toast the slices of bread until they are charred and crisp on the outside but still feel springy to the touch when pressed. Lightly rub one side of each slice with the garlic clove, spread a thin layer of stracchino on top, distribute the crushed broad bean and pea mixture evenly, and add a twist of black pepper. Cut each slice in half and finally finish with a good drizzle of olive oil and the scattered lemon zest.

MINESTRA ALLA GENOVESE

For 4 to 6

There are so many different types of minestrone soup that I found it difficult to get to the bottom of which is most authentic. This certainly seems to be the most popular in Venice and there is a good historical reason behind its favor. The Republic of Genoa effectively occupied the Venetian Republic at the end of the fourteenth century after 150 years of conflict, and while there may not have been a great deal of unity then, it seems some of the culinary traditions persist.

This is a vibrant and summery soup, delicious even when served cool on hot days.

1 large head of Swiss chard
extra virgin olive oil
1 large onion, peeled and thinly sliced
2 celery stalks, thinly sliced
2 leeks, washed, trimmed, and sliced
2 carrots, peeled and cubed
2 heaping teaspoons gremolata (see page 301)
flaky sea salt
2 large waxy potatoes, peeled and cubed

2 zucchini, cubed
2 large handfuls of fresh borlotti beans, podded
a large handful of green beans, trimmed and halved
2 large handfuls of fresh peas, podded
freshly ground black pepper
4–6 tablespoons pesto (see page 299)
5¼ ounces Parmesan, grated, to serve

Cut off the muddy bottom of the chard head and discard. Wash and dry the leaves. Cut the stalks into bite-size pieces and slice the leaves. Set aside.

Place a very large saucepan over a medium heat and add a few generous glugs of olive oil. Gently sauté the chard stalks, onion, celery, leeks, and carrots for about 8 minutes, until they are soft and glossy. Add the gremolata and a good pinch of salt, stir for a minute, then add the potatoes, zucchini, borlotti, and green beans. Stir once or twice, then add enough water to just about cover the ingredients, but do not completely submerge them. Bring to a boil, then reduce to a simmer and leave the soup bubbling gently for half an hour.

Add the peas and the chard leaves and simmer gently for an additional 5 minutes. Taste, season with salt and black pepper if necessary, and ladle into warmed soup bowls, finishing each with a tablespoon of pesto. Serve with the grated Parmesan and crusty bread.

LOBSTER *and* FENNEL SOUP

For 4

Despite the heavyweight ingredients, this is a light, summery soup with delicate flavors, perfect on its own for a simple lunch. I suppose we associate lobster with indulgence and luxury, but its flesh has a subtle quality, particularly when coupled with subtle bedfellows. The reason I use vegetable rather than seafood stock is to emphasize the aniseed flavors of the fennel and tarragon. This is given further clout by the addition of Pernod, sambuca or kümmel. This makes a large batch for four people; from experience, I always go back for seconds.

2 medium fennel bulbs
1 large onion, peeled
extra virgin olive oil
flaky sea salt
1 large potato, peeled and diced
½ teaspoon celery seeds

½ teaspoon fennel seeds
8½ cups vegetable stock (see page 304)
1 lobster, approx. 2¼ pounds
¼ cup Pernod, sambuca, or kümmel
a small handful of tarragon, chopped

De-core the fennel and remove and retain the delicate, feathery fronds. Set them to one side. Chop the fennel roughly and slice the onion. Heat a good glug of olive oil in a very large saucepan. Gently sauté the onion and fennel for about 5 minutes, until glossy and translucent. Add a pinch of salt, the diced potato, and the celery and fennel seeds and stir a few times to incorporate everything.

Pour in the stock, turn up the heat to high and bring to a boil. Partly cover with a lid and reduce to a gentle simmer for about 45 minutes.

Meanwhile, bring a separate very large pan of water to a boil and cook the lobster for 12 to 15 minutes.

Allow both the fennel soup and the lobster to cool. Cut open the lobster with a very sharp knife, break the claws with nutcrackers or the end of a rolling pin, and remove as much flesh as possible. Dice. Transfer the soup to a blender and whiz it to a smooth consistency.

Return the soup to the saucepan, add the Pernod (or what have you) and tarragon, bring to an enthusiastic simmer for a few minutes, and test the seasoning. Add salt if necessary. Remove from the heat.

Incorporate the lobster into the soup, stir a few times, divide equally among warmed bowls and garnish with the retained fennel fronds.

MUSSEL SOUP

For 4

I had the great privilege to accompany a small fishing expedition out into the lagoon one morning to examine the mussel beds near the tiny island of Campalto. The beds are all privately owned, I was told, but I couldn't quite get my head around it. How can anyone own part of the lagoon? Does the ownership correspond to fishing rights or are there title deeds? No matter. It seems that there is a healthy respect for whose beds are whose and there is a great deal of honor among fishermen.

The beds are all in very shallow parts of the lagoon, so expert navigation is critical. And the mussels we collected were huge, some 4 inches in length. I was given a few pounds and went home to make this hearty and fragrant soup, based roughly on instructions from one of the fishermen. I was very happy with the results.

4½ pounds mussels
2¼ pounds very ripe tomatoes
extra virgin olive oil
2 cloves of garlic, very finely sliced
a large handful of basil leaves, torn
flaky sea salt

a glass of white wine
¾ cup plus two tablespoons fish stock (see
page 305)
freshly ground black pepper
a large handful of breadcrumbs
(see page 300)

Scrub the mussels in cold running water and set aside. Discard any that are open.

Boil a kettle and place the tomatoes in a large heatproof bowl. Pour the boiling water over them and leave for 2 minutes. Carefully drain and, when the tomatoes are cool enough to handle, slice the skin lengthwise with a very sharp knife. You should be able to pop them out easily. Discard the skin.

Cut the skinned tomatoes in half, remove the seeds, and finely chop the flesh. This will produce quite a lot of juice, which you should retain.

Heat a good couple of splashes of olive oil in a very large saucepan and gently sauté half the garlic for about 2 minutes. Don't let it burn. Add the chopped tomatoes and half the basil with a very good pinch of salt and turn up the heat. Continue to stir, allowing the mixture to bubble, until the tomatoes have disintegrated and you are left with a thick sauce. This will take about 10 minutes.

Meanwhile, warm another few glugs of olive oil in a separate large saucepan for which you have a lid, and gently sauté the remaining garlic for 2 minutes before adding the mussels. Turn up the heat to high, stir, then add the wine and allow to evaporate. Now add the stock and cover with the lid. Cook for about 2 minutes, until all the mussels have opened. Discard any that have not. Remove from the heat and allow them to cool enough for you to handle them.

Put half the mussels into the saucepan of tomatoes. Remove the other half from their shells and put these in too, but not the shells. Add a good twist of black pepper and the remaining basil. Stir and bring up the heat until just bubbling, adding a little of the leftover stock from the other pan if needed to loosen the soup, then take off the stove. Taste and adjust the seasoning if necessary. Divide equally among four warmed bowls, scatter over the breadcrumbs, drizzle with olive oil, and serve with plenty of crusty bread.

FENNEL, MINT, *and* ORANGE SALAD

For 4

The fennel bulbs I buy from Stefano on Via Garibaldi are about the size of a small fist, but have fronds that extend upward so that they sometimes protrude from the top of my shopping basket. This is in contrast to the fennel found on supermarket shelves, which tend to be neatly trimmed and polite. I prefer the unruly version because the herby extensions come in very handy for recipes like this one. Raw fennel is such a great ingredient, particularly when sliced very thinly; the intense licorice flavor can sometimes take you by surprise.

1 fennel bulb
2 navel oranges (or blood oranges in spring)
1 small red onion, peeled
a large handful of good black olives
extra virgin olive oil
flaky sea salt
a small handful of mint leaves

Cut the fennel in half lengthwise and remove and discard the core. Cut off a few of the feathery fronds and set them aside. Using a mandoline with safety guard or an extremely sharp knife, slice the fennel very thinly indeed.

Peel the oranges and separate the segments. Set 2 segments aside. Use a sharp, serrated knife to remove the pith and the membrane from the others.

Slice the onion as thinly as possible and remove the pits from the olives by squeezing them between thumb and index finger—it doesn't matter if they get squashed in the process.

Put the fennel, orange, onion, and olives into a very large mixing bowl and add a generous glug of olive oil and a good crunch of sea salt flakes. Sacrifice the 2 reserved segments by squeezing their juice into the bowl and discarding them. Turn once or twice, add the mint leaves, turn once more, and divide equally among four pretty plates, garnishing each with the reserved fronds.

FRESH SPAGHETTI *with* RAW PEAS, YOUNG PECORINO, *and* MINT

For 4

Peas are best eaten raw. Everyone knows that. If you have to cook them, you should do so only briefly, in a gentle sauté, and then only with good reason. Risotto is an exception. When I read recipes telling me that frozen peas will do, I often find myself shouting, "No, they will not."

I do adore the immediacy and rawness of this dish, with everything made from scratch and the salty freshness that a ewe's milk cheese such as Pecorino brings to the ensemble. A tip on the Pecorino: buy it young, not aged, and when grating, do not apply too much pressure. It is better to have light, fluffy gratings that will give the dish a lot more delicacy and subtlety.

12 ounces fresh pasta dough (see page 302)
"00" flour, for dusting
10½ ounces fresh peas in their pods, podded
*   to yield 5 ¼ ounces peas*
a handful of small, delicate mint leaves

¼ cup (½ stick) butter
the zest and juice of ½ a lemon
3½ ounces young Pecorino, finely grated
flaky sea salt
freshly ground black pepper

Using a pasta roller on its widest setting, pass the dough through twice. Bring it down a notch and pass it through twice more. Fold the sheet back on itself and pass it through twice again, back on the widest setting. Repeat this, always passing twice and going down a notch at a time, until the pasta dough is about the thickness of a coin.

Alternatively, you could achieve this with diligent rolling, using a well-floured wooden pin on a large, floured work surface. Once flat, cut the ribbons as thinly as possible, around 10 inches in length, with a large, very sharp knife.

If you're using a pasta machine, pass the dough through with the spaghetti attachment and carefully lay down the 10-inch spaghetti strips on a floured surface, or, as I see frequently in my neighbors' kitchens, over the back of a chair.

Separate the peas, putting the very small ones into a bowl and the remainder into a large mortar. Roughly pound with a pestle, but do not pulp. Mix them back together and set aside. Slice the mint leaves into very thin ribbons.

Bring a large pot of salted water to a boil and cook the spaghetti for no more than 2 minutes. Retain a small cup of the pasta cooking water and drain the spaghetti. Put a large, deep-sided frying pan over medium heat and melt the butter. Add the lemon juice, then the drained pasta. Turn up the heat, stir, and remove from the stove. Distribute over most of the grated Pecorino, the mint, the lemon zest and a good pinch or two of salt. Turn over a couple of times with tongs to incorporate everything, adding a splash of the retained starchy water. Serve on four warmed plates, scattering over the remaining Pecorino and finishing with a twist of black pepper.

SPAGHETTI CASSOPIPA

For 4

Antiche Carampane in the old red light district of Venice is one of the city's best restaurants. It is family-run and has an uncompromising attitude to the quality of its cooking and the provenance of its dishes. Often, the only voices you hear in the dining room are Venetian (not even Italian), making it feel very local and clubby. No bad thing.

Francesco, the owner, is fond of telling me about the history of the dishes he brings to the table. This is my version of one of his most celebrated pasta dishes. It originates from Chioggia, a fishing town on the southern edge of the lagoon, and was traditionally made with leftover fish from the bottom of the net, flavored with mild spices—a reminder that Venice was for many centuries the gateway between east and west on the spice route.

10½ ounces mussels
10½ ounces clams
10½ ounces razor clams
extra virgin olive oil
2 cloves of garlic, peeled and halved
4 heaped tablespoons soffritto
* (see page 303)*
2 fillets of red mullet, skinless
flaky sea salt

a glass of white wine
ground cinnamon
grated nutmeg
1 sprig of thyme
1 bay leaf
½ cup passata (tomato purée)
1 pound spaghetti
a small handful of flat parsley,
* finely chopped*

Scrub the shellfish, discarding any that are open, and soak in cold clean water for an hour or two. Drain and set aside.

In a very large, deep-sided frying pan, heat a few good glugs of olive oil and very gently sauté the garlic. When it starts to brown, remove and discard. Add the shellfish to the pan and turn up the heat, stirring for a minute or two. As soon as the shells have opened, remove from the heat. Discard any that have not.

The clams and mussels will have released quite a lot of liquid, so strain them through a sieve over a clean bowl and reserve the cooking juices. When cool enough to handle, carefully remove all the clams and mussels from the shells, place on a board, roughly chop, and set aside.

Pour a few glugs of olive oil into a large, heavy-bottomed saucepan and sauté the *soffritto* over a low heat for about 10 minutes, until soft and translucent. Add the red mullet with a good pinch of salt, turn up the heat a little, and continue to fry for an additional couple of minutes, turning once. Pour in the wine. When it has evaporated, add a good pinch of cinnamon, a pinch of grated nutmeg, the thyme sprig, bay leaf, and half the retained shellfish cooking juices. Allow the sauce to bubble away for a couple of minutes, then add the chopped shellfish and the passata. Add more of the reserved shellfish cooking juices if necessary to create a silky sauce.

In a large pot of salted boiling water, cook the spaghetti according to the package's instructions minus 1 minute. Drain and transfer to the heavy-bottomed saucepan. Remove the sprig of thyme and the bay leaf, add the chopped parsley, and incorporate fully over a low heat for 1 minute, adding a little more of the reserved juices if the sauce needs loosening.

Serve while steaming hot.

BUCATINI *with* SARDINES *and* SCALLIONS

For 4

I am occasionally prone to obsessive urges and one morning before a day of cooking I had a thought I couldn't shake: when a recipe requires a pan of salted water, what does that mean? Most Italian chefs and home cooks I canvased said the same thing—as salty as the sea.

So, in the spirit of adventure and in the interests of culinary science, I got the vaporetto to the Lido, went to the Adriatic coast, and filled a plastic bottle with sea water.

Back in my kitchen I set about testing my sample against tap water with varying amounts of table salt dissolved in it, using the tip of my tongue as my scientific salinity gauge. The answer was particularly pleasing. One heaping teaspoon (about ¼ ounce) of salt per 4¼ cups of water tastes exactly as salty as the Adriatic Sea.

This dish is a really fresh and light lunchtime favorite, the texture of the bucatini the perfect balance to the deliciously soft sardines. Don't be tempted to use spaghetti or linguine here; they're too limp.

16 small sardines, gutted, filleted, tailed, and decapitated
12 ounces bucatini
extra virgin olive oil

a large bunch of scallions, finely sliced, green bits too
flaky sea salt
a large handful of basil leaves, torn
freshly ground black pepper

Separate the 8 smallest fish and roughly chop the 8 largest. Set aside.

Bring a large pot of salted water to a boil and cook the bucatini according to the package's instructions minus 2 minutes.

Heat a few glugs of olive oil in a very large, deep-sided frying pan and gently sauté the scallions with a good pinch of salt. Stir for 5 minutes, until the onions are soft, glossy, and translucent.

Place the small whole sardines in the pan with the scallions and carefully cook for 2 minutes each side. When the pasta is almost done, retain a cup of the cooking water, drain, and transfer the bucatini to the large frying pan. Add the chopped fish and stir thoroughly. Throw in the torn basil leaves, loosen with a little of the reserved pasta water if needed, stir once more, and serve on warmed plates with a generous drizzle of olive oil and a twist of black pepper.

San Pietro di Castello

There is a beautiful walk from the end of Via Garibaldi to the island of San Pietro di Castello. When I need solace, and want to feel grass and soil beneath my feet rather than the relentless *maségni*—those Istrian stone paving slabs that make up most of the city's streets—I will head to the church there, a little oasis of calm and greenery. The route passes through the easternmost tip of Castello, along the Sant'Anna Canal and over the Ponte di Quintavalle. Sometimes, I will take this route and not see a single soul. Other times I will pause on the bridge and watch the scant activity at the boatyard where water taxis go for repair, or wait for a *batellina* to pass below—an antique wooden boat in which the rider stands, facing forward, with two long oars, practicing the local rowing technique known as the *voga*.

Once I'm on the small island of San Pietro, the atmosphere changes again and becomes even quieter and more serene. There are only fourteen interconnected streets and a handful of dwellings, some social housing, and a few medieval buildings, particularly around the church. I love the names of the streets and have memorized the *nizioléti*, the black and white signs painted directly onto the render of corner buildings, using the standard stenciled capital letters required by the commune of Venice. There is Corte Nova, Ramo del Zoccolo, Campiello dei Pomeri, Fondamenta Olivolo and, improbably, Calle del Casino. Was there really once a casino on this humble and chaste island? One sign that always catches my eye is the painted number above a rather grand, Moorish doorway on Calle Quintavalle. In Venice, door numbers are not geographically sequential, but tend to be allocated in a scattershot, hodgepodge manner. Additionally, they designate buildings in the entire district, not just the street. This place is number 1. You really don't see it that often. There are only six "number ones" in the whole city, the most famous of which is the Doge's Palace.

The church of San Pietro di Castello was Venice's cathedral up until 1807. (Before that, the current cathedral, the Basilica of St. Mark, was a private chapel for the use of the Doge and his cohorts.) It sits in its own *campo*, a local word that describes a square, usually with a well at the center. In the rest of Italy this would be called a *piazza*. (In Venice, there is only one *piazza*—St. Mark's—and everything else is a *campo*.) The word literally translates as "field"—they were originally small grass pastures with livestock. All have now been paved over, with one exception: Campo San Pietro. This is my sanctuary, a place where I can sit on one of the red benches, read a book, or close my eyes and listen to the sparrows squabbling in the autumn or the swifts circling and squealing in the spring skies above. I find the rare abundance of grass and trees quite therapeutic; it's odd how we covet that which is scarce.

There is a beautiful hidden courtyard within the church with some crumbling façades, wonky doorways, and an olive tree. It is so quiet that the only thing I can hear when I stand there is my own breathing. Outside, the impressive bell tower, like many in Venice, leans at an alarming angle, probably at 86 degrees or 87 degrees rather than a perpendicular 90 degrees. This is the third tower to be built here— the other two collapsed. Curiously, on the paved path between the trees in the *campo*, there is a single white cobblestone. This is not an anomaly. It was placed there for a very good reason. When San Pietro was the city's cathedral, its patriarch would have received the Doge for special services and important religious occasions. For the Doge to be welcomed ceremoniously by the patriarch would have created certain hierarchical difficulties—neither wanted to be seen as less important than the other. A diplomatic compromise was reached and the two would meet discreetly, and quite unceremoniously, on the precise spot designated by the white stone.

SPAGHETTINI *with* OVEN-DRIED TOMATOES, CHILE, *and* GARLIC

For 4

There is a scene in the Martin Scorsese movie *Goodfellas* where a few jailed gangsters are making a *ragù* in the prison kitchen. One of the cons uses a razor blade to slice the garlic so thinly that you can see through it. Such is his dedication to the sauce that the blade is being used to cook rather than to cut throats or effect an escape.

Likewise, this sauce requires the garlic to be sliced extremely thinly. Additionally, it distinguishes itself by not requiring Parmesan as an ingredient, something that you may find counterintuitive if, like me, you tend to put it on everything. Resist the temptation.

1 pound spaghettini
10 oven-dried tomatoes (see page 202)
2 cloves of garlic, peeled
extra virgin olive oil

flaky sea salt
1 teaspoon dried chile flakes
about 30 basil leaves
freshly ground black pepper

Bring a large pot of salted water to a boil and cook the spaghettini according to the package's instructions minus 1 minute. Retain a cup of the starchy cooking water and drain. While the pasta is boiling, chop the oven-dried tomatoes and slice the garlic cloves extremely thinly, using a very sharp knife.

Heat a few glugs of olive oil in a very large frying pan and gently sauté the sliced garlic with a pinch of salt for about 2 minutes. Add the chopped oven-dried tomatoes with the chile flakes and a few pinches of salt, and stir for another minute. Now turn up the heat, add the drained spaghettini and the basil leaves, incorporate everything very well, using a little of the retained pasta cooking water if necessary, and remove from the heat.

Mix once more and serve on four warmed plates, with a drizzle of olive oil and a twist of black pepper.

PEA, CHANTERELLE, *and* ASPARAGUS RISOTTO

For 4

I make no apologies for my preoccupation with peas. No other vegetable has the same elegance and significance at this time of the year. Additionally, there is such freshness to their flavor and texture that rarely a day goes by between the months of April and July without me grabbing a handful of raw peas as a snack. The classic *risotto primavera* is well known, but this is a hearty version that I sometimes prefer because of its earthiness and depth of flavor. The addition of lemon zest at the end affords a lovely zing and freshness.

6⅓ cups vegetable stock (see page 304)
extra virgin olive oil
2 medium white onions, peeled and
    finely diced
1 small celery stalk, peeled and finely diced
flaky sea salt
1¾ cups Carnaroli rice
a glass of dry vermouth
8 slender asparagus spears, woody stalk
    ends discarded

10½ ounces fresh peas in their pods, podded
    to yield 5¼ ounces peas
5¼ ounces chanterelles
⅓ cup (5⅓ tablespoons) unsalted butter
a large handful of grated Parmesan,
    about 1½ cups
a few pea shoots
the zest of 1 lemon
freshly ground black pepper

Heat the stock in a large saucepan and keep it simmering. Put a couple of glugs of olive oil in a separate large, heavy-bottomed saucepan and place over low heat. Gently sauté the chopped white onions and celery with a good pinch of salt. Continue for 15 minutes or so, making sure they do not color or stick. They will take on a glossy, translucent appearance. Add the rice and mix well, coating each grain. Turn the heat up a little and add the vermouth. This will produce a satisfying hiss of steam and a beautiful aroma.

Add a ladleful of hot stock and gently stir. Continue to do so slowly and gently, making sure the mixture never absorbs all the liquid and is always very slightly submerged. Add more stock, little by little, and repeat for the next 12 minutes.

Meanwhile, cut the asparagus spears into 1½-inch sections, then halve them lengthwise. Mix into the risotto and stir gently for another 5 minutes, slowly adding more stock as necessary. Add the peas and chanterelles. Stir well, but carefully, so as not to crush the mushrooms. Cook for another 4 to 5 minutes, then test the rice for doneness. It should have a little resistance between your teeth but should not be hard. Remove from the heat. Add the butter and the Parmesan, folding them carefully into the risotto until fully absorbed, and serve on warm plates with a garnish of pea shoots and a very light scattering of lemon zest and black pepper.

LINGUINE *with* CLAMS *and* RAPINI

For 4

I allow myself the occasional moment of excitement at the morning market when *rapini* appears. Sometimes called *cime di rape* ("turnip tops" in English) and broccoli rabe, this plant is a wonderful ingredient on its own but heroic in partnership. Although it is most famous in the regional signature dish of orecchiette in Puglia, Venetians love it too. Visually it looks a little like the leaves of a broccoli plant with tiny florets between the stems, but its flavor is tantalizingly bitter. Combined here with clams it creates that magical *agrodolce* profile—sweetness from the bivalves, bitterness from the plant.

10½ ounces small clams
extra virgin olive oil
1 clove of garlic, very finely chopped
a small glass of white wine
1 pound linguine
a large bunch of rapini, thick stalks removed and discarded
flaky sea salt
a small handful of flat parsley leaves, chopped
chile flakes

Wash the clams with a hard brush in cold running water. Discard any that are open.

Bring a large pot of salted water to a boil for the linguine.

Heat a very generous glug or two of olive oil in a large, heavy-bottomed saucepan for which you have a lid. Sauté the garlic for 30 seconds and then add the clams. Turn up the heat, stir a few times, then add the wine. When the cloud of steam starts to subside, cover with a lid and return the heat to medium. At this point, put the linguine into the boiling water and cook according to the package's instructions.

Turn your attention back to the clams and, after 3 minutes, add the *rapini*, shake a few times, cover the pan, and continue cooking for 5 additional minutes, until all the clams have opened. Discard any that do not open. Drain the pasta, having first retained a cupful of the starchy cooking water. Add the drained linguine to the clams with a good pinch of salt, the parsley, and a flourish of chile flakes, and turn the heat to low. Stir well to incorporate the *rapini* and clams with the linguine, adding a splash or two of the reserved pasta water. Serve in warmed bowls with a hunk of crusty bread and an extra dish for the empty clam shells.

AGED PARMESAN RISOTTO

For 4

Much has been written about umami, the mysterious fifth flavor that sits alongside the more familiar sweet, sour, bitter, and salty. It's not as easy to define as the famous four, but most of us can identify it when we taste it. It contributes unctuousness, roundness, and mouthfeel when it is present and usually makes you want to eat more. Parmesan cheese is one of its best-known exponents, so its ubiquity in Italian cooking is unsurprising; it makes just about everything taste better. What *is* unusual is to see Parmesan as a main ingredient. This risotto requires really excellent-quality aged cheese, so do buy the best you can afford.

6⅓ cups chicken stock (see page 304)
⅓ cup (⅔ stick) butter
1 large white onion, very finely chopped
flaky sea salt
1¾ cup Carnaroli rice
a small glass of dry vermouth
5¼ ounces excellent aged Parmesan, finely grated
freshly ground black pepper

Heat the stock in a large saucepan at the back of the stove and keep it simmering, ladle at the ready. Melt half the butter in a large, heavy-bottomed pan over medium heat and add the onion with a few pinches of salt. Sauté until glossy and translucent, turning frequently with a wooden spoon, then add the rice. Make sure each grain is coated and the onion and rice are fully incorporated.

Now, pour in the vermouth, enjoy the pungent cloud of boozy steam, and when the liquid has almost all evaporated, add one ladle of stock and stir. Repeat this for the next 15 minutes, carefully adding the stock a small ladleful at a time, never allowing the rice to fully dry out but not waterlogging it either.

When the rice is almost done, but still has a bit of bite (test a grain between your front teeth), add a final splash of stock, the remaining butter, and turn up the heat. Stir vigorously for 30 seconds and remove from the stove. Add most of the Parmesan, stir once or twice, and cover. Rest for a full minute before serving on warm plates. Scatter over the remaining Parmesan and garnish with a twist of black pepper.

ZUCCHINI, MINT, *and* GOAT'S CHEESE RISOTTO

For 4

With a natural predisposition to Parmesan, it is easy to see how other types of cheese might be overlooked as cooking ingredients in Italian cuisine, but I absolutely love the subtle tang that a good goat's cheese can impart to a dish. In this instance, it marries beautifully with zucchini and mint, resulting in a risotto that is not just elegantly textured and creamy, but also a little more subtle; perfect for a light lunch on a warm day.

6⅓ cups vegetable stock (see page 304)
extra virgin olive oil
a large bunch of scallions,
*   very finely sliced*
flaky sea salt
1¾ cups Carnaroli rice
a glass of Sauvignon Blanc

2 medium zucchini
5¼ ounces excellent goat's cheese
a large handful of mint leaves,
*   roughly chopped*
a large knob of butter
freshly ground black pepper
the zest of ½ a lemon

Heat the stock in a large saucepan and put it to simmer at the back of the stove with a ladle handy. Pour a few good splashes of olive oil in a separate large, heavy-bottomed saucepan and place over a low heat. Very gently sauté the scallions with a good pinch of salt for 10 minutes or so, until they are soft and glossy, but not brown. Add the rice and mix well, coating each grain. Turn the heat up a little and pour in the wine. This will produce a satisfying hiss and a beautiful smell.

Add a ladleful of stock and stir. Continue to do so slowly and gently, making sure the rice never absorbs all the liquid but is always just submerged. Add more stock, little by little, and repeat for the next 8 minutes.

Trim the zucchini and cut into quarters lengthwise. Slice the long pieces at an angle to create 1-inch triangular chips about ¼ inch thick. Mix them into the risotto and stir gently for another 6 minutes, slowly adding more stock as necessary. Crumble half the goat's cheese and mix in, along with the mint. Stir well, cook for another 4 minutes or so, then test the rice for doneness. It should have a little resistance between your teeth but not be hard. Adjust the seasoning at this point if necessary.

Remove from the heat. Add the butter and remaining crumbled goat's cheese and fold carefully into the risotto until fully absorbed. Cover and rest for a minute, then serve on warmed plates with a twist of black pepper and a very light scattering of lemon zest.

SPINACH *and* RICOTTA MALFATTI

For 4

I am not a show-off in the kitchen. I am not a professional chef and my technique tends to have that clumsy inelegance that distinguishes home cooks from the restaurant variety. But when there is fun to be had in the kitchen, I do like to share it.

These malfatti (literally "badly made") are so-called because they too, like me, are clumsy and inelegant. But the method of getting them to that state involves swirling a wine glass above your head in a slightly eccentric manner. Children love it and I have even had dinner guests helping me. That way, everyone gets to share the blame when the wonky dumplings come to the table, shimmering in that delicious butter and sage sauce.

1 pound baby spinach leaves, washed
⅓ cup "00" flour
1 cup ricotta
1 large free-range egg, beaten
2½ cups grated Parmesan
flaky sea salt

freshly ground black pepper
½ teaspoon freshly grated nutmeg
1¼ cups semolina
7 tablespoons butter
a handful of picked sage leaves

Steam the spinach for 3 minutes, then drain away the excess water and chop the leaves very roughly. Set aside. Mix the flour and ricotta in a large bowl until it resembles lumpy, moist breadcrumbs. With a wooden spoon, stir in the egg and three-quarters of the Parmesan. Add a good pinch of salt, a decent twist of pepper, the nutmeg, and the spinach, and combine everything thoroughly.

Take a large, stemmed wine glass and drop in a tablespoon of semolina. Using a separate, clean tablespoon, dollop a glob of the mixture into the glass. Swirl around for a few seconds until you have a walnut-size dumpling. Place on a generously semolina-dusted tray. Repeat until all the mixture is used up. When you have finished, you should have 24 or so little malfatti.

Fill a large pot with cold water and bring to a hearty boil. Drop in the malfatti as quickly as possible, bring back to the boil, then continue to simmer for about 3 minutes.

Meanwhile, in a small saucepan over medium heat, melt the butter and add the sage leaves. When it bubbles, reduce the heat to very low.

The malfatti will float to the surface when they are ready. Turn off the heat, remove the malfatti with a slotted spoon, and drain the excess water on a clean tea towel. Evenly distribute among four warmed plates, pour the butter and sage over the top, and finally scatter over the remaining Parmesan.

PIZZA MARINARA

For 1

This is the original pizza. Tomato, garlic, olive oil, oregano. No mozzarella and no embellishments. I have seen it with anchovies but this is an error that unfortunately persists. I'm sorry, but it is wrong. Marinara refers to a simple sauce that was favored by seafarers and has nothing to do with fishy ingredients.

Like many classics, it is perfect as it is as long as you use an excellent tomato sauce, slice the garlic as thinly as possible, and take care that it doesn't burn. It even works very well with garlic oil and dried oregano if you find yourself without the fresh stuff.

1 tangerine-size ball of pizza dough (see page 301)
plain flour, for dusting
2 tablespoons tomato sauce (see page 300)
½ a clove of garlic
1 teaspoon oregano leaves
extra virgin olive oil
flaky sea salt

Preheat the oven as high as it will go. Put in a pizza stone if you have one, or a baking sheet, to heat up.

Stretch and roll the dough out on a floured surface until it is a rough disk of around 9 inches or so. If the sides are slightly uneven, all the better. Try to leave the edges a little thicker.

Using the back of a large spoon, spread the tomato sauce evenly over the pizza base, stopping ½ inch from the edge.

Slice the garlic as thinly as you possibly can. Scatter the garlic and oregano over the surface of the pizza.

Place the pizza directly on the stone or on a hot baking sheet. This one will cook in about 4 to 6 minutes, so keep an eye on it and remove it when the edges are starting to turn dark brown, but before the garlic turns golden brown.

Finish with a drizzle of olive oil and a pinch of salt.

FRIED PIZZETTA MARGHERITA

For 4

I have very few memories of my maternal grandfather, who died when I was a toddler, but I do remember the occasion he let me try some of his fried bread. I guess it would have been a slice of farmhouse white finished off in the same pan used to fry his bacon and eggs.

Fried pizza is just as memorable, and although it isn't something you might want to eat every day, it is a really comforting variation on a familiar Italian classic. It also uses the stovetop and broiler rather than the oven, so I find it an easy, convenient, and swift way to get your pizza fix.

1 tangerine-sized ball of pizza dough (see page 301)
plain flour, for dusting
olive oil (not extra virgin)
6 tablespoons tomato sauce (see page 300)
1 large ball of buffalo mozzarella
a small handful of basil leaves
flaky sea salt

Divide the dough into four equal pieces. On a floured surface, stretch, roll and flatten each piece into a rough wonky disk with slightly thicker edges, about a hand's span in diameter. Leave the dough to rest for 15 minutes.

Preheat the broiler to its highest setting. Heat around ¾ inch of olive oil in a large, deep-sided frying pan, and fry each dough disk for 1 minute, turning once. Replenish the oil if necessary.

Carefully place the fried pizzette on two large baking sheets and smear with the tomato sauce, stopping ½ inch from the edges. Break up the mozzarella into small pieces and distribute evenly with the basil leaves. Add a trickle of olive oil and a pinch of salt to each, place under the broiler for a few minutes, and remove when the edges are starting to turn crisp and brown and the mozzarella has melted.

BUTTER-FRIED JOHN DORY

For 4, as a starter

This is a dish I have never seen in a restaurant. One of my neighbors makes it for her children with non-flaky white fish, but there is no reason you couldn't try it with anything that cuts into finger shapes when raw. I like John Dory because the fillets are uneven, resulting in wonky fingers, and it has a robust, nutty flavor. Using melted butter to shallow-fry is quite common among older northern Italian home cooks, some of whom still look upon olive oil as something foreign, having originated in southern Italy. It certainly adds to the richness.

It won't have escaped your notice that this is effectively a recipe for fish fingers. I suppose that's why children like them.

4 John Dory fillets, medium
1 ½ cups "00" flour
3 large eggs, beaten
1 cup (2 sticks) unsalted butter
fine salt
1 lemon

Wash the fillets and dry well. Carefully cut each one into three, lengthwise, to create long finger shapes.

Take three bowls. Put half the flour into bowl number one, the beaten eggs into bowl number two, and the remaining flour into bowl number three. Dip each strip of John Dory in sequence in bowls one, two, and three (flour, egg, flour), then set aside.

To clarify the butter, melt it over a medium heat in a small saucepan. Scrape the foamy scum off the top and, very carefully, transfer the remaining golden liquid to a frying pan, leaving behind the dark deposits at the bottom of the saucepan.

Turn the heat up a little under the frying pan that now contains the clarified butter and, when it just starts to bubble, fry the battered John Dory fillets in batches for about a minute each side, until they have turned golden brown. Drain well and blot on paper towels. Sprinkle generously with salt while hot and serve with a wedge of lemon.

SWEET *and* SOUR SLIP SOLES

For 4, as a starter

As a seafaring nation, thirteenth-century Venice had to devise ways of feeding its sailors often several days or weeks after they had set sail. The technique of preserving lightly fried sardines in vinegar with the addition of sautéd onion and dried fruit and nuts is a wonderful example of necessity as the mother of invention. In one neat package, most of the essential food groups are covered, including, crucially for sailors, onions: high in vitamin C and perfect for keeping scurvy at bay. The dish is extremely tasty and it is still made exactly the same way today. Most fish can be prepared in this style, from sardines to mackerel, prawns to the slip soles (small Dover soles) below. The dish tastes better after a few days and is always eaten at room temperature.

8 small slip sole fillets, skinned
1 ½ cups "00" flour
extra virgin olive oil
flaky sea salt
4 large white onions, sliced
a small handful of raisins

a small handful of pine nuts
¼ cup superfine sugar
a glass of white wine vinegar
a glass of white wine
freshly ground black pepper

Make sure the slip soles are cleaned and dried, dredge them in flour, then lay them in a very large frying pan in which you have heated 1 inch of olive oil over high heat. Fry for 2 minutes or so, turning them once or twice, until they are nicely golden brown. Rest the fried soles on paper towels and sprinkle generously with salt while they are hot.

Using the same pan, turn the heat down to medium-low, add a splash more olive oil if necessary, and gently sauté the onions for 15 minutes, until translucent and soft but without browning them at all. Add the raisins, pine nuts and sugar and stir a few times. Now pour in the vinegar and the white wine, and turn the heat up to allow the mixture to bubble for a few minutes. When the onions look glossy and yield when pressed with a wooden spoon, remove from the heat and allow to cool a little.

Lay 4 of the soles in the bottom of a large, pretty serving dish (preferably one for which you have a lid). Pour over just under half the onion mixture, to cover the fish. Now lay the last 4 soles on top and finish by pouring over and layering the remaining onion mix so that the fish are fully covered. Add a twist of black pepper, put the lid on, and leave in the fridge for 24 to 48 hours.

Make sure you remove the dish from the fridge half an hour before you are ready to serve. Traditionally eaten with a slice of grilled polenta (see page 171).

RAZOR CLAMS

For 4

This may well be my favorite dish at Alle Testiere, the tiny but celebrated fish restaurant in the heart of Venice's historic center. The razor clams available in Rialto Market are beautiful, so small and delicate, around one quarter of the size they are in the UK, where they are often referred to as "spoots." I remember telling Luca di Vita, the co-owner of the restaurant, about the large razor clams we get in the British Isles. "Yes, we have those type, too," he said. "But we use them as bait." He was teasing, of course—this dish works just as well with British spoots as with lagoon razors.

The quantities below are for normal portion sizes. I enjoy these delicious bivalves so much that I often make more than I think I need. They always get eaten.

3.3 pounds very small razor clams
extra virgin olive oil
2 cloves of garlic, peeled and
    very finely chopped
flaky sea salt

a large glass of white wine
a large knob of butter
a small handful of flat parsley leaves,
    chopped
1 lemon, halved

Make sure the clams are all closed, then wash them in cold running water, scrubbing any sand, mud, or seaweed off with a clean scouring pad. Dry them.

Over high heat, warm a very good glug of olive oil in a large, heavy-bottomed saucepan for which you have a lid. Add the garlic and sauté for 30 seconds, then tip in all the clams. Carefully turn them a few times, add a pinch or two of salt, then add the wine. Allow the pan to bubble fiercely for 30 seconds, then reduce the heat to medium, cover with the lid, and leave until the clams have all opened, about 4 to 6 minutes, depending on their size. Discard any that have not opened.

Using two large spoons, transfer the clams to a very large, warmed serving plate. Pour the juices from the pan through a very fine strainer into a smaller saucepan. Place it over high heat and add the butter, the chopped parsley, and the juice from one of the lemon halves. Reduce the sauce for around 30 seconds, until it becomes a little syrupy, pour over the clams, quarter the remaining lemon half, and distribute with a hunk of crusty bread and a glass of cold Soave.

SWORDFISH PUTTANESCA

For 4

Puttanesca is the classic store-cupboard sauce, traditionally knocked up in a sluttish manner with whatever you find in the pantry, but these days it is a lot more prescriptive and contains more than a fair share of salty ingredients to add punch and piquancy. My version is stripped back and minimalist, more of a salad than a sauce, but all the better on a summer's day because of it.

Now, swordfish at Rialto Fish Market is plentiful and often the fishmongers there will display a swordfish head or a glorious marlin as a trophy. But I am aware it jumps on and off the endangered list with frequency, so please do check and feel free to substitute sustainable tuna steaks instead, equally delicious with this tangy accompaniment.

40 (or so) ripe cherry tomatoes
flaky sea salt
12 tinned anchovy fillets
20 Kalamata olives
2 cloves of garlic, crushed
2 tablespoons small capers

a small handful of oregano leaves
freshly ground black pepper
extra virgin olive oil
4 swordfish steaks
20 (or so) basil leaves

Slice the tomatoes in half and lay them on a chopping board, cut side up. Season generously with salt flakes and leave to stand for 5 minutes. Roughly chop half the anchovies. Pit the olives by squeezing the pits out between finger and thumb—don't worry if you squash them, they're better like that.

Put the tomatoes, chopped anchovies, olives, garlic, and capers into a very large mixing bowl with the oregano, a pinch of salt, a good twist of black pepper, and a few glugs of olive oil. Turn over once or twice with your hand and leave to stand.

Meanwhile, warm an oiled grill pan over high heat, season each side of the swordfish steaks, and grill for about 3 to 4 minutes each side. If you don't have a grill pan, you could simply pan-fry the seasoned steaks in a frying pan with a little olive oil. (The grill gives such lovely grill lines, though.)

Place the swordfish onto four warmed plates, divide the puttanesca sauce equally over the steaks, scatter the basil leaves haphazardly, and distribute the remaining anchovy fillets.

SEA BASS IN CRAZY WATER

For 4

The term *acquapazza*, which translates as crazy water, refers to the poaching liquid in this dish, a combination of herbs, tomatoes, capers, chile, and wine, lending a zingy, fresh piquancy to the soft white flesh of the sea bass. If you can't get small fish, try cooking one very large bass in your biggest pan and simply putting it, lock, stock, and barrel, in the center of the table. It makes for more of a visual centerpiece and helps the meal feel more like a feast.

4 small whole sea bass, gutted (ask the fishmonger to do this)
extra virgin olive oil
1 clove of garlic, very finely sliced
1 red chile, deseeded and finely chopped
flaky sea salt
1 pound ripe cherry tomatoes, halved
a glass of white wine
a full handful of capers
a small handful of flat parsley leaves, chopped
a small handful of basil leaves, torn

Check that your gutted fish are free from remnants of their innards and wash thoroughly under cold running water. Pat them thoroughly dry.

In a very large, high-sided frying pan for which you have a lid, heat a good glug of olive oil over medium heat and carefully lay the fish side by side. Sprinkle over the garlic, chile, and a good pinch or two of salt. After 4 minutes, gently turn the fish over and add the halved tomatoes, making sure they are nicely coated and incorporated into the cooking juices. Leave to sizzle for another 4 minutes. Now add the wine and capers, cover, and simmer for a further 4 minutes, until the fish is cooked through. You can check by piercing the flesh at the thickest part of the body. The eyes will have turned white, too.

Carefully lay the fish on four warmed plates. Add the chopped parsley and basil to the pan, turn up the heat for a minute or two to reduce the tomatoes, capers, and sauce to a syrupy consistency, and spoon on to the four sea bass.

MASHED BROAD BEANS
with GREMOLATA

For 4, as a side dish

Side dishes are largely absent from trattoria menus in the city, particularly those authentic local canteens like Dalla Marisa. It is a concession to tourists, I suppose, that you will find side salads, fried potatoes, and steamed vegetables in restaurants with an international clientele. But in residential kitchens they are nonexistent.

The fact that I still like a side of veg with my main course, then, is a sign that I haven't fully assimilated into Venetian life. This broad bean mash is a favorite.

4¼ pounds fresh broad (fava) beans in their pods,
  podded to yield 2¼ pounds beans
flaky sea salt
freshly ground black pepper
extra virgin olive oil
½ a clove of garlic, peeled
a small handful of flat parsley leaves
the zest of ½ a lemon
a large knob of butter

Bring a large saucepan of salted water to a boil and add the broad beans. Cook for about 5 minutes, then drain and rinse under a cold tap until cool enough to handle. Using your thumbnail, pierce the membranes and pop the broad beans out one by one. It's a laborious process but one that I find quite therapeutic. Discard the skins.

Place all the double-podded broad beans back into the empty saucepan with a few pinches of salt, a twist of black pepper and a glug of olive oil. Using a potato masher, mash the beans into a rough paste. You may prefer to do this in batches in a mortar and pestle. Either way, make sure the mashed beans end up back in the saucepan and set aside.

To make the gremolata, use a very sharp knife and chop the garlic as finely as you can. Do the same with the parsley. Place in a small bowl with the lemon zest and mix together thoroughly.

Put the mashed broad beans back on medium heat and stir with a wooden spoon until they start to loosen and steam. Taste and add more salt if necessary. Add the knob of butter, stir until it has melted, then transfer to a large serving bowl with the gremolata scattered over the top.

AMALFI LEMONADE

Makes a generous jug for 2

On summer days when the breeze drops and the sun is high in a cloudless sky, it can be difficult to find respite from the heat and humidity in Venice. July and August can get stiflingly hot, and since I don't have air-conditioning I have to find other ways to cool down. Going for a swim in the Adriatic on the far coast of the neighboring island of the Lido is one way; making a large jug of lemonade is another.

This recipe was given to me by my friend Will Skidelsky (although his mother Gus might take credit for passing it on to him) and, as long as you stick to the exact proportions, it works every time. I try to always make mine with Amalfi lemons from the market, but good quality organic, unwaxed lemons will give excellent results, too.

For the lemonade:
1 Amalfi lemon
4 tablespoons superfine sugar
5 large cubes of ice
2½ cups water

To serve:
lots more ice
a few sprigs of mint

Cut the lemon in half, and put it into a food blender with the sugar, ice cubes, and water. Make sure the lid is tightly on and whiz for 20 seconds.

Fill a large jug with ice and, using a sieve, strain the blended lemon mixture into the jug. Stir once or twice and serve in tumblers, garnishing with a little mint.

MY GIN MARTINI

For 1

Venice has more than its fair share of hard-drinking alumni. Ernest Hemingway, Orson Welles, and Burton and Taylor may not have ever clinked each other's glasses in the city but they certainly were among its most famous imbibers. One thing unites them, however, and that is the Gin Martini.

As Hemingway was fond of telling anyone who would listen, a Martini must be very cold and very dry. His favored proportions were 15:1 gin to vermouth, which he called a "Montgomery," supposedly after Field Marshal Bernard Law Montgomery (1887–1976), who was said to like the same odds in battle. My version lingers at the stirring stage, which introduces a third essential ingredient: water.

2 teaspoons dry vermouth
2½ ounces excellent gin
1 unwaxed lemon

Fill a cocktail shaker with ice. Pour in the vermouth, stir for about 15 seconds so that the vermouth coats the ice cubes, then strain the vermouth away. Remember, for the magic 15:1 ratio, you only need ¾ teaspoon of vermouth to remain in the drink and the coated ice cubes will now do this trick.

Add the gin and, using a long-handled bar spoon, stir in one direction only for about 30 seconds. This part of the process is important for two reasons—it chills the drink very quickly and effectively, and it also allows a little dilution from the ice, an essential ingredient in a classic Martini.

Strain into a chilled antique 5-ounce Martini glass and, using a very sharp knife or a speed peeler, shave a large, single lozenge of skin from the lemon (no flesh or pith) and carefully twist it over the surface of the drink to release the oil. You should see a few drops of oil floating on the surface. Run the twist around the rim of the glass and drop it in. Serve and drink immediately.

BELLINI SORBET

For 4

Giuseppe Cipriani, the founder of Harry's Bar, had a thing for Venetian painters. When he created a dish of sliced, raw beef, the deep red color reminded him of the pigment favored by the artist Vittore Carpaccio, and so beef carpaccio was born. Similarly, when attempting to re-create the soft, pale pinks so often seen in Giovanni Bellini's paintings, he turned to peaches. The resulting cocktail, Cipriani's most famous creation, has immortalized the artist's name so that the majority of the world associates it with the drink rather than with Venice's greatest painter.

This startlingly simple recipe is my reinterpretation of the famous cocktail as a dessert. It is a delight on a summer's day and avoids the need for an ice-cream making machine, something I don't possess in any case. Try to use white peaches if you can find them—they are so much more fragrant and delicate than the yellow-fleshed variety. You need to prepare this a day in advance.

6 ripe white peaches
2 tablespoons honey
2 tablespoons superfine sugar
1 cup very cold prosecco, and more for serving

Halve the peaches lengthwise, remove and discard the pits and the skins, slice each half into four segments, and lay on parchment paper on a freezer-proof tray. Freeze overnight.

Put the honey into a small saucepan with 2 tablespoons of water and place over medium heat. Stir and add the sugar, bringing to a gentle bubble, but not a boil. Set the syrup aside.

Place the frozen peach pieces in a blender with the prosecco and the cooled honey syrup, blend until smooth and consistent, then scoop into chilled wine glasses with a splash of cold prosecco on each.

ALMOND CAKE

For 8

One of the chief pleasures of mornings in Venice is taking a stroll to buy a small loaf of bread or some pastries and stopping for a swift coffee or two. The venerable *caffè* Rosa Salva on Campo Santi Giovanni e Paolo is a good example, but my favorite cake shop is Rizzardini near Campo San Polo. Established in 1742, it's a family affair, run by Paolo and his daughter Marta. The pastries are super, but I tend to go for the little cakes. They have an almond slice I particularly like. Here's my rather more homely version, perfect with a milky coffee as a morning treat.

butter, for greasing
4 medium eggs
⅔ cup superfine sugar
1⅓ cups ground almonds
¼ cup potato flour
the zest and juice of 1 lemon
5 teaspoons amaretto
a large handful of sliced almonds

Grease an 8-inch springform cake pan with butter and preheat the oven to 350°F/180°C.

Separate the eggs, placing the yolks in a very large mixing bowl and the whites in a medium bowl. Add the superfine sugar to the yolks and beat until pale and smooth. Now gradually incorporate the ground almonds and flour, the lemon zest, lemon juice, and amaretto, beating to create a thick, consistent mixture.

Take the bowl of egg whites and whisk them enthusiastically into stiff, fluffy peaks. Now, carefully fold them into the almond mixture and incorporate well.

Transfer the mixture into the greased cake pan, evenly scatter the sliced almonds, and place in the oven for 40 to 45 minutes. Test for doneness by pushing a steel skewer into the center of the cake—it should come out dry.

Allow the cake to cool for 10 minutes, then transfer to a wire cake rack. Serve warm with a handful of fresh raspberries as a dessert or with an espresso for a mid-morning indulgence.

NECTARINES *with* WALNUTS, ROSEMARY, *and* GORGONZOLA

For 4

The old Italian folk saying, "Don't tell the peasants that pears taste delicious with cheese," might derive from estate owners trying to diskourage seasonal fruit pickers from eating the crop for lunch with a hunk of Pecorino, or it could be apocryphal. Either way, the sense is the same: cheese and fruit are a match made in heaven. The natural sugar from ripe nectarines and the salty tang from Gorgonzola are just wonderful here, and I've added a layer of aromatics with the rosemary syrup and a satisfying crunch with the roasted walnuts. This summery dessert is so versatile, you could even serve it as a starter.

2 handfuls of walnut halves
3 tablespoons honey
2 plump sprigs of rosemary
2 tablespoons superfine sugar
6 ripe nectarines
4¼ ounces Gorgonzola dolce, rind removed

Preheat the oven to 350°F/180°C and scatter the walnuts on a baking tray. Dry roast for 10 minutes or so, until they are starting to darken and smell warm and nutty. Remove and allow to cool.

Put the honey and 2 tablespoons of water into a small saucepan with the rosemary and place over medium heat. Bring the mixture to a gentle bubble but do not allow it to boil. Stir in the sugar and let it dissolve. When the syrup is loose and incorporated, remove from the heat, discard the rosemary, and allow to cool completely.

Cut the nectarines in half lengthwise and remove the pits. Cut each half into four segments and carefully place in a large mixing bowl. Add the cooled syrup and gently turn over a few times with a wooden spoon. Break the toasted walnuts roughly between your fingers and thumb, add to the bowl, and turn over once more.

Transfer to four wide plates, then break the Gorgonzola into small pieces and distribute evenly.

CHOCOLATE, HAZELNUT, *and* NOUGAT SEMIFREDDO

For 6

Ice cream is so firmly associated with Italian cuisine that semifreddo is often over-looked. This is a shame because I prefer it to ice cream and it is much easier to make. This particular semifreddo is similar to what I usually order at my favorite ice cream shop in Venice, Nico. There, they cut a thick slice from a block and stuff it into a glass filled with freshly whipped cream. They then cover the tip of this chocolate iceberg with even more whipped cream. It's known as *gianduiotto* and I urge you to try one next time you are in Venice. Sitting outside Nico with one of these on a summer's day with a view of the Guidecca Canal is as good as it gets.

½ cup hazelnuts
2 cups plus 2 tablespoons double cream
10½ ounces excellent dark chocolate,
    70% cocoa, chopped

4 medium eggs
⅓ cup plus 2 tablespoons superfine sugar
butter
3½ ounces hard nougat, finely chopped

Heat the oven to 350°F/180°C and scatter the hazelnuts onto a baking sheet. Place in the oven for 6 to 8 minutes, until turning brown and smelling toasty and nutty. Remove, allow to cool enough to handle, then wrap the nuts in a kitchen towel and rub them vigorously. This will remove their skins. Transfer to a mortar and pestle and bash briefly to break them into rough pieces. Set aside.

Take three bowls, two of which must be of the ovenproof Pyrex variety and the right size to fit onto the top of a saucepan.

Put the cream into the non-fitting bowl. Put the chocolate into the second bowl and the eggs into the third, along with the sugar. Butter a large loaf pan and line it with plastic wrap.

Bring a saucepan half full of water to a boil. Reduce to a simmer, then place the bowl of sugar and eggs over it and whisk vigorously until doubled in volume. Immediately remove from the heat and place the bottom of the bowl in very cold water. Continue to whisk until the mixture is cool. Set aside.

Place the bowl with the chocolate in it over the saucepan and turn up the heat. Melt the chocolate, turning it with a wooden spoon. When fully melted, fold it into the egg and sugar mixture. Add the hazelnuts and the nougat.

Now, using a clean whisk, whip the cream until it forms soft, fluffy peaks, and fold it into the chocolate and egg mixture. Pour the combined mixture into the loaf pan, smooth the surface with a palette knife, and leave for half an hour. When it is completely cool, cover with plastic wrap and place in the freezer for at least 24 hours and up to a week.

Twenty minutes before you are ready to serve, remove all plastic wrap, turn out onto an attractive serving dish, and place in the fridge. This allows the semifreddo to soften and become "semi-cold", hence the name. Cut into ¾-inch slices with a very sharp knife warmed gently under the hot tap, and serve on chilled plates.

AUTUMN CELERY SALAD • ROASTED RED CHICORY • TUNA, RADICCHIO, AND HORSERADISH CROSTINI • CAVOLO NERO BRUSCHETTA • RIBOLLITA • FISH SOUP • GNOCCHI WITH SAGE AND BUTTER • RAVIOLI DI MAGRO • BLACK RISOTTO • PICKLED CUCUMBER • POLENTA • GRILLED POLENTA WITH CHOPPED OLIVES AND ANCHOVIES • GRILLED POLENTA WITH WILD MUSHROOMS AND GARLIC • WHIPPED SMOKED MACKEREL ON GRILLED POLENTA • WET POLENTA WITH BROWN SHRIMP • PAN-FRIED SEA TROUT, SALICORNIA, LEMON BUTTER • VEAL "QUAIL" KEBABS • ROASTED PORK INVOLTINI WITH PROSCIUTTO AND GARLIC • STUFFED ROAST PORK ROLL (PORCHETTA) • LITTLE CABBAGE BUNDLES • FRIED MEATBALLS • MEATBALL SPIEDINI WITH SAGE • LITTLE "LOST BIRD" KEBABS • ROASTED SQUASH WITH TOASTED SEEDS AND SAGE • VENETIAN POTATOES • OVEN-DRIED TOMATOES • SWEET AND SOUR ROASTED ONIONS • GIBSON • OLIVE OIL CAKE • LEMON POLENTA CAKE • FRIED CUSTARD • PISTACHIO LOAF

AUTUMN

"Cauliflower is nothing but cabbage with a college education."
Mark Twain

The Most Serene Republic of Venice was created by decree at 12 noon on March 25, 421 in the church of San Giacomo near Rialto Bridge. It became a maritime state in 1204, and a landed state in 1400. In the sixteenth century, Venice further asserted its presence on the world stage by resisting the combined efforts of feudal and monarchist Europe to subsume it and by sticking to its federal, republican roots. It had become a mighty city state.

La Serenissima ruled itself majestically for the next two centuries, a paragon of peace, effective governance, and a center of art, music, theater, craftsmanship, and hard-earned wealth. That all came to an end with the arrival of Napoleon in 1797. Then began its loss of independence, its dissipation, the various Austrian and French occupations, its decline, and its fall. Finally, after the construction of the ironically named Liberty Bridge, connecting the island of Venice to mainland Italy in the middle of the nineteenth century, the once-great republic effectively became a region in the House of Savoy's Kingdom of Italy.

No wonder Venetians are proud.

In twenty-first-century Venice that pride is still fiercely evident in many ways. It manifests itself politically among the various separatist and isolationist groups who want to return Venice to its independent past with its own sovereignty. You can hear it every day in the distinct accent and impenetrable dialect that residents often use to speak to one another. You can even see it in the street signs, the *niziolét*i, which are frequently vandalized (or "corrected") if sign writers use double hard consonants, Ts and Ds mostly, since those don't exist in Venetian dialect. The prominence of the gold and red flag depicting the winged lion of St. Mark is a strong visual indicator as you walk around the city and frequent its bars and restaurants.

But the loveliest manifestation of pride is found in the markets. Here, traders display food from all over Italy: tomatoes from Sicily, tuna from the north Atlantic, sea bass from the Adriatic. When fruit, vegetables, fish, or seafood come from the lagoon, or the nearby island of Sant'Erasmo, or a farm just beyond Treviso, however, it's different. These items are marked *nostrani*: "ours." This is particularly evident when the seasons offer up an ingredient that has just come onto the market. The stallholders' pride isn't born of nationalism or regional prejudice, it is simply that they are proud to be selling local produce, farmed, harvested, reared, or caught by local fishermen, farmers, and artisans. Needless to say, it makes me want to buy all the produce that is *nostrani*, too.

There is another quirk in the market signs and labels that I rather enjoy and that is the use of dialect. Octopus, universally *polpo* in Italian, is *folpo* in Venice. Peas are *piselli* everywhere on the mainland, but *bisi* in Venice. Even the delicate soft-shell crabs from the lagoon are *moleche* in other parts of Veneto, but *moeche* here in Rialto.

In autumn, I delight at the arrival of radicchio, the knobbly acorn squash from Montebelluna, and the exquisitely dappled pink and pale yellow lettuce from Castelfranco. This season is short in Venice because summer bleeds well into September and winter starts in earnest in November, but while autumn lasts, the markets glow with golden hues and ochre shades. The days may be shorter, but the change to the quality of light is remarkable. At the golden hour, those long moments before the sun sets, the light is almost liquid—molten and gilded—and time becomes elastic, seeming to stretch and play tricks on simple minds like mine, completely seduced by the magic this season conjures. There is a beautiful and dramatic effect on home cooking, too, as it takes on many of the season's characteristics.

After a summer of vibrant salads and fresh flavors, autumn is also the time of the year when my thoughts turn to pasta making. There are many kitchen activities I find soothing and therapeutic (you can read about my meditative approach to soffritto on page 303), but I have to say, making pasta is at the top of that list. In Venice, pasta is always made on the kitchen work surface, never in a bowl, and I follow that approach, too. It tends to give the process a ceremonial feel, as if everything has to stop while this important ritual begins. Cracking eggs into a well made of flour and then bringing the flour into the middle with a fork feels more like playtime in the nursery than serious cookery, and I have found the freedom to spill, scatter, and spread with abandon actually helps to make the pasta freer and looser. I tend to roll with a wooden pin rather than use a classic chrome pasta roller, and I would encourage you to try this traditional method—it is quite liberating.

AUTUMN CELERY SALAD

For 4

Quite often, my plans for a particular day's meal will change completely if I see something at the market that catches my eye. One morning in early October I was struck in particular by some immense bunches of celery. The leaves were so abundant and fragrant that I took that as my starting point.

I find that supermarket celery is often trimmed, so using the leaves is not an option, but they have a remarkable flavor and are vastly underrated. Try to find the bushiest, most verdant bunch when shopping at the greengrocer.

a large handful of shelled walnuts
3 celery stalks, leaves intact
2 fennel bulbs
1 large, ripe Comice pear
the juice of 1 lemon
extra virgin olive oil
flaky sea salt
freshly ground black pepper
3½ ounces Parmesan

Preheat the oven to 350°F/180°C. Scatter the walnuts on a baking tray and roast for 6 to 8 minutes, until they are starting to brown and smell toasty. Remove and set aside.

Remove the leaves from the celery, wash and dry, then roughly chop and set aside. Peel the celery sticks and slice them at an angle. Trim the fennel, quarter the bulbs, then remove and discard the core. Slice very thinly. Now peel the pear, halve it lengthwise, remove the core, and slice thinly, also lengthwise.

Carefully place the celery, fennel, pear, and celery leaves in a very large mixing bowl. Add the toasted walnuts, crushing them lightly with your fingers as you do. Evenly drizzle over the lemon juice, with a good glug of olive oil, a hearty pinch of salt flakes, and a twist of black pepper. Very gently turn the salad over in the bowl with your hand, then transfer equally to four large bowls or wide plates.

Lastly, using a very fine microplane grater, distribute a generous amount of Parmesan onto each serving with a scant splash of olive oil and a final flourish of ground black pepper.

ROASTED RED CHICORY

For 4

One of the things I miss most when I leave Venice is radicchio. It is an ingredient so important to Venetian cooking that it is a constant presence in the markets and on the dinner table from October to April. But back in Blighty it can be harder to find. Red chicory, however, is much easier to get hold of, and I sometimes cheat when I crave that bitter tang by roasting it rather than using it as a salad. It is from the same family and, with the application of heat, offers up that distinctive soft bite and the ability to excite the tongue. Some of the outer leaves might burn and char if your oven is doing its job, but please don't be afraid of this—it adds flavor and texture.

4 red chicory heads
extra virgin olive oil
flaky sea salt
freshly ground black pepper
Parmesan, for serving

Preheat the oven to 375°F/190°C.

Cut each chicory head in half lengthwise. Put a splash or two of olive oil onto a large baking tray and place in the oven for 5 minutes. Remove the tray and put the chicory halves, cut side down, on the tray. Lightly coat their backs with a drizzle of oil and return to the oven. Reduce the temperature to 325°F/160°C.

After 8 to 10 minutes, turn the chicory halves over and season with salt and pepper. Replace into the oven for an additional 8 minutes.

Serve hot, with freshly grated Parmesan.

TUNA, RADICCHIO, *and* HORSERADISH CROSTINI

A bar snack for 4

Al Merca, a tiny hole-in-the-wall spritz bar next to Rialto Market, is a magnet for locals, tourists, and market traders, all seeking midday refreshment. There is barely enough room for a cat, let alone to swing it, but the crowds spill out onto the large open *campo* and the atmosphere is often raucous. The food on offer is basic—meatballs and small crusty rolls— but one of their sandwiches is, in my opinion, the star of the show. Pairing canned tuna with horseradish was a small stroke of genius. I prefer to smother the mixture onto warm toasts.

1 small head of radicchio (Treviso tardivo if you can)
1 small (5 or 6 ounce) can of tuna in olive oil
4 generous teaspoons creamed horseradish (from a jar)
½ cup mayonnaise
flaky sea salt
½ a loaf of sourdough bread
extra virgin olive oil
freshly ground black pepper
a small piece of fresh horseradish, for grating

Chop the radicchio into small pieces, discarding the stalk. Wash and dry, then place in a large mixing bowl.

Add the tuna, including the oil, the horseradish from the jar, and the mayonnaise and mix thoroughly with a wooden spoon. Add a few pinches of salt.

Cut the sourdough into ½-inch-thick slices, rub with a little olive oil, and toast under a broiler until golden brown. Cut the crusts off and create 8 rectangular lozenges, around 3 inches x 2 inches.

Spread the tuna and radicchio mix on the crostini, add a twist of black pepper, and finish with a drizzle of olive oil and a grating of the fresh horseradish.

CAVOLO NERO BRUSCHETTA

For 4

Black cabbage, or black kale, is now a common ingredient and I couldn't be happier about that. It's a deeply delicious brassica with a multitude of applications. It starts to appear on the market stalls in Venice in autumn, and although the really coarse, hearty variety isn't available till later in the year, after the first frost, I prefer the delicate leaves of the early ones.

2 small heads of cavolo nero
4 large slices of sourdough or Pugliese, ¾ inches thick
1 clove of garlic, peeled and halved
freshly ground black pepper
flaky sea salt
extra virgin olive oil

Remove the leaves from the cabbage heads and discard the cores and the stems. This can be done easily by holding the stalk firmly with one hand and pulling in the opposite direction with the other. Cut the leaves into rough, wide strips.

Bring a large saucepan of salted water to the boil and gently boil the cavolo nero for 12 to 15 minutes, until very tender. Drain well and allow to cool. Squeeze out any excess water with your hands. Thoroughly chop the cooked leaves and set aside.

Grill or toast the slices of bread until they are charred and crisp on the outside but still feel springy when tweaked between finger and thumb. Rub one side of each slice with garlic, distribute the cavolo nero evenly, and add a twist of black pepper and plenty of sea salt flakes. Cut each slice in half and finally finish with a good drizzle of olive oil.

RIBOLLITA

For 4

So often, domestic Italian recipes call for stale bread, usually chopped or torn into small chunks and sometimes soaked in milk. It is this frugal, sensible approach to household management that characterizes the cooking I love and certainly informs the choices of home cooks in Venice, always with one eye on the purse strings.

Ribollita is a great example of a hearty dish that, despite its humble, inexpensive ingredients, does not compromise on flavor. The addition of the bread creates a texture that I find deeply comforting, too. Perfect to slurp away those late-autumn blues.

1⅔ cup dried cannellini beans
2 bay leaves
extra virgin olive oil
1 large onion, finely diced
1 large carrot, finely diced
1 large celery stalk, finely diced
1 clove of garlic, finely chopped
flaky sea salt

1 teaspoon fennel seeds, crushed
a small handful of thyme leaves
freshly ground black pepper
1 14.5 ounce can of diced tomatoes
½ a loaf of stale bread, crustless,
    torn into small chunks
1 whole cavolo nero, roughly shredded

Soak the beans overnight in a very large bowl with one of the bay leaves and plenty of cold water.

Next day, drain the beans, transfer to a large pot, and cover well with fresh cold water. Bring to a boil, then reduce to a simmer for 30 minutes, until soft. While cooking, remove scum as it comes to the surface. Retain 2 large cups of the cooking water, drain the beans and set aside.

In a large, heavy-bottomed saucepan, heat a good glug or two of olive oil and gently sauté the onion, carrot, celery, and garlic for a good 15 minutes, until soft and glossy. Add a good pinch or two of salt, the crushed fennel seeds, the thyme, and a twist of black pepper.

Now add the chopped tomatoes, the cooked beans, one of the cups of cooking water and the second bay leaf, and stir over medium heat for about 30 to 45 minutes. About halfway through, submerge the chunks of stale bread in the soup and add the shredded cavolo nero. You may need to use the second cup of cooking water.

When done, your thick soup will improve vastly if you leave it overnight in the fridge and reheat it the next day (*ribollito* means "reboiled"). Either way, remember to remove the bay leaves and finish each bowl with a twist of pepper and a drizzle of olive oil.

FISH SOUP

For 4

There are as many recipes for fish soup in Italy as there are days in the year. And they vary dramatically, too. I have had fantastic lobster broths in Sicily, tomato-rich soups around Naples, and a rather vinegary version in Chioggia. The one essential ingredient, always, is the stock. It must be rich and homemade. There really are no shortcuts.

This is a rather easy, pared-down version that borrows a little boozy flourish from classic French bisque. You can, of course, use any white fish for the central ingredient, but I really like the meaty texture of monkfish and it is usually quite easy to get hold of. Take your time making this; a little patience and a leisurely pace will allow the flavors to develop and integrate. Crusty bread is the only accompaniment you need.

extra virgin olive oil
4 heaping tablespoons soffritto (see page 303)
flaky sea salt
½ a clove of garlic, finely chopped
7 ounces squid, cleaned
2 large monkfish tails
2 fillets of red mullet
16 large prawns or shrimp, shelled

a glass of white wine
¾ cup passata (tomato purée)
6⅓ cups rich seafood stock (see page 305)
3½ tablespoons Vecchia Romagna (or other brandy)
a handful of flat parsley leaves, chopped
freshly ground black pepper

Pour a good few glugs of olive oil into a very large saucepan and place over medium heat. Gently sauté the *soffritto* with a good pinch of salt for around 10 minutes, until soft and translucent. Add the garlic for the last minute.

Meanwhile, cut the squid into bite-size pieces, quarter the monkfish tails and halve the mullet fillets. If the prawns are very large, cut them in half lengthwise, small ones leave whole.

Add the squid only to the *soffritto*, sauté for a few minutes, then add the white wine. When the wine has evaporated, add the passata, stir, pour in the stock, and bring to a gentle simmer.

Continue to simmer very gently for about half an hour, until the soup has reduced by about a quarter. Carefully place the remaining fish in the soup, stir very gently, and simmer for a further 5 minutes, until the broth has poached the fish pieces. One minute before taking off the heat, test the seasoning, adjust if necessary, and stir in the Vecchia Romagna.

Ladle the soup into deep, warmed bowls and distribute the fish evenly. Finish with a drizzle of olive oil, a scattering of chopped parsley, and a twist of black pepper.

GNOCCHI *with* SAGE *and* BUTTER

For 4

Make no mistake, this is a classic, and with very good reason. Italian cooking has certain foundation blocks on which the whole canon is built, and if you dare to mess with those, the result can be disastrous. One of the reasons this dish is so revered is that it's a sort of triple-whammy combination of comfort: pasta, potatoes, and butter. I defy anyone not to be seduced by the aromas, flavor, and mouthfeel afforded by well-made gnocchi in a simple butter and sage sauce.

If you're feeling ambitious, gently score the individual gnocchi with the tines of a fork before cooking. This creates tiny ridges which help them retain a little more of the buttery sauce at the table. Delicious.

1¾ pounds floury potatoes, not too large
1½ cups "OO" flour, plus more for dusting
fine salt
1 nutmeg
3 large egg yolks
7 tablespoons butter
1 shallot, peeled and very finely sliced
flaky sea salt

1 clove of garlic, peeled and very
*   finely sliced*
a large handful of sage leaves,
*   stalks removed*
a small glass of white wine
1½ cups grated Parmesan
freshly ground black pepper

Bring a large pot of salted water to a boil and cook the potatoes, whole, for about 20 minutes, until a skewer can be pushed easily into the center without too much resistance. Drain them, then, when they are cool enough to handle, peel and put into a potato ricer. Squeeze directly and evenly onto a floured work surface. Discard the skins.

Season the remaining flour with a good pinch or two of fine salt, sift it over the potatoes, and grate about half the nutmeg evenly over the flour. Create a well in the middle, a little bit like a shallow volcano, and add the egg yolks. Use a fork to bring the flour and potato mix into the middle, then work into a soft dough, kneading a little until smooth.

Roll the dough with your hands and divide into 4 equal pieces. Create 4 long sausage shapes, about ½ inch thick, then, using a blunt knife, subdivide each sausage into ¾-inch sections. You should have created about 28 little rectangular dumplings. If there are more, save them for later.

In a very large, deep-sided frying pan, melt the butter over medium heat and gently sauté the shallots with a good pinch of flaky sea salt for 5 minutes, until soft and translucent but not browned. Simultaneously, bring a large pot of salted water to a boil. Add the garlic and sage leaves to the frying pan with shallots and butter and sauté for another minute or two, until the leaves are just starting to crisp. Pour in the wine.

When the water is boiling, drop in the dumplings. You may need to do this in batches. When they float to the top it means they are ready. Remove them with a slotted spoon and transfer them to the frying pan of sage and butter. Stir several times and remove from the heat. Scatter most of the Parmesan over the gnocchi and turn over once. Transfer to four warmed plates, equally distributing all the buttery sauce. Finish with a twist of black pepper and the remaining Parmesan.

RAVIOLI DI MAGRO

For 4

Just a little north of Campo Santa Maria Formosa there is a fascinating and unique bookshop called Libreria Acqua Alta. It is run by Luigi Frizzo, a multilingual eccentric ex-miner who stores his many hundreds of thousands of books in canoes, bathtubs, and a full-size gondola, all within the shop, to help protect them during Venice's frequent high-tide floods.

Luigi knows I'm interested in cookery books and will occasionally thrust something at me: "Look at this—I think you will like it." One book he sold me, an old tome on household management that, oddly, smelled of apples, contained this fourteenth-century recipe, which actually turned out exceptionally well. The translation is something like "lean ravioli," possibly because it contains no meat, and the white pepper gives the dish a distinctive spiciness.

1⅓ pounds baby spinach leaves, thoroughly washed and drained
1¼ cups ricotta
5¼ ounces Parmesan, grated
7 tablespoons very soft butter

fine salt
ground white pepper
1 pound fresh pasta dough for ravioli (see page 302)
freshly ground black pepper

Start by cooking the spinach in boiling salted water for 3 minutes. Drain and squeeze out all the moisture. (Spinach retains so much water you may need to do this a few times.) Chop the spinach thoroughly into a paste and put it into a large mixing bowl with the ricotta, two thirds of the Parmesan, half the butter, and a good pinch of salt and white pepper. Mix thoroughly with a fork to fully incorporate all the ingredients and set aside.

Make sure your pasta dough has reached room temperature and roll it out on a floured work surface. Make it as thin as possible, then, using an 3-inch circular pastry cutter (or even a large wine glass), cut as many circles as you can. Roll the remaining dough together, flatten again into a thin sheet and you should get a few more circles.

Using a tablespoon, place a generous dollop of the spinach and ricotta mixture in the center of each dough disk and press the edges together to create little semicircular half-moon shapes.

Bring a large pot of salted water to a boil, carefully place the ravioli in the water and cook for no more than 3 minutes. Remove, drain, and transfer to a clean warm bowl. Add the remaining butter and gently turn the ravioli to coat them. Transfer to four warmed plates, scatter over the remaining Parmesan, and some freshly ground black pepper and serve.

BLACK RISOTTO

For 4

There are some ingredients that leave you in no doubt as to their provenance. The nutty flavor of Spanish pata negra ham, for example, betrays the acorn diet of the black-footed pigs from which the meat comes. English asparagus has a deep and distinct grassy tang that gives away its heritage with a single bite. And I always think of cuttlefish as synonymous with the sea. It is so unambiguously flavored by the ocean that any dish containing it is transformed. The shiny black ink only serves to emphasize the otherworldliness of the creature, but it also gives this risotto an added layer of creaminess and a wonderful velvety texture.

1 pound cuttlefish
6⅓ cups vegetable stock (see page 304)
extra virgin olive oil
1 medium onion, peeled and finely chopped
1 leek, washed, trimmed, and
    finely chopped
1 clove of garlic, peeled and very
    finely chopped

flaky sea salt
1 cup dry vermouth
4 packets of squid ink (½ ounce)
1¾ cup Carnaroli rice
a small handful of flat parsley leaves, chopped
freshly ground black pepper
the zest of 1 lemon

First, remove the central blade of the cuttlefish, its eyes, mouth, outer membrane, and any hard parts. Inside you will find its ink sacs—remove these carefully and set aside. Discard all the other bits. Rinse thoroughly under cold running water until white. You should be left with the tube of the body, the empty head, and the tentacles. Cut all into large, bite-size pieces.

Pour the stock into a saucepan and keep it simmering gently at the back of the stove. Heat 2 tablespoons of olive oil in a large, heavy-bottomed frying pan and gently sauté the chopped onion, leek, and garlic with a good pinch of salt for a few minutes, until just starting to brown. Now add the cuttlefish and brown that, too. Keep stirring to make sure it doesn't stick. Add half the vermouth, stir until it has evaporated, then add the cuttlefish ink from the sacs, the squid ink, and a ladleful or two of stock. Reduce to a simmer, cover, and leave on low heat for 15 minutes.

In a separate large saucepan, heat 2 tablespoons of olive oil over medium heat and add the rice. Stir to coat each grain until it has just started to toast, then add the remaining vermouth. It will steam and evaporate quickly. Add a ladleful of stock, reduce the heat to low, stir, and continue to add more stock every time the rice starts to dry out, for about 12 minutes.

Pour in the cuttlefish mixture, stir, and continue to cook for another 8 to 10 minutes, adding a little stock at a time to make sure the risotto never dries out. Test a grain between your teeth, and when done, add more salt if necessary, stir in the chopped parsley, add a twist of black pepper, and serve in warmed bowls with a scattering of lemon zest.

PICKLED CUCUMBER

For 4, as a side

I like to make a batch of this in advance and keep it in the fridge. It will happily stay in the marinade for a week, but in my experience it rarely lasts that long. Cold and crunchy, it is a delicious accompaniment to simply grilled sardines, or those lovely marinated white anchovies from the deli counter. My favorite use for it, however, is as a foil to the whipped smoked mackerel on grilled polenta recipe on page 176. It's that combination of tangy fish and sharp pickle that is so winning on a sunny autumn day. You need to prepare this at least a day in advance.

1 tablespoon fennel seeds
2 medium cucumbers
½ cup extra virgin olive oil
½ cup red wine vinegar
⅓ cup superfine sugar
flaky sea salt
freshly ground black pepper
a small handful of chopped oregano leaves

Place a small frying pan over medium heat and toast the fennel seeds until they are just starting to brown and beginning to smell warm and nutty. Set them aside.

Cut the ends off the cucumbers and then, using a speed peeler, slice them lengthwise into thin, flat ribbons. Lay the strips in a lidded heatproof plastic container.

Put the olive oil and red wine vinegar into a saucepan with the sugar and whisk thoroughly. Add a good pinch of salt and a twist of black pepper. Place over medium heat and, continuing to whisk, warm the mixture but do not boil. Allow to cool slightly. Scatter the fennel seeds and oregano over the cucumber ribbons, then pour the warmed oil and vinegar into the container. Make sure the cucumber is fully submerged, cover, and leave in the fridge for at least 24 hours.

When ready to serve, shake off any excess liquid and lay in folds on a serving plate.

POLENTA

For 6

It is sometimes difficult for non-Italians to understand polenta. It's a sort-of porridge and school-dinners-era-semolina hybrid and it does take a little effort in use and presentation to make it palatable, let alone exciting. But once you have been initiated and enlightened to its versatility, it reveals itself, works its magic, and eventually welcomes you with open arms into the cult.

The two most common styles of polenta are soft (with butter and Parmesan) and grilled. The former is delicious as an accompaniment to sauced meats, the latter as a base for creamed salt cod.

8 ½ cups water
flaky sea salt
2 cups polenta flour or coarsely ground cornmeal
extra virgin olive oil (for grilled polenta only)
2 ¼ cups Parmesan, grated (for wet polenta only)
¾ cup (1 ½ sticks) butter, softened (for wet polenta only)
freshly ground black pepper

Bring the water to a boil with a good pinch or two of salt. Put the polenta flour into a large jug with a spout to make it easier to pour. Reduce the heat to bring the water to a simmer. Very slowly introduce the polenta flour in a steady stream while stirring clockwise with a wooden spoon. When the polenta and water are fully mixed, it will bubble up alarmingly. Reduce the heat to low and continue to stir clockwise, slowly, for about 40 minutes. The polenta is ready when it falls away from the sides of the pan. Season generously.

For grilled polenta, pour the mixture onto a large wooden board (or even the center of a clean kitchen table—very Venetian) and allow it to cool completely. It will naturally spread like lava and solidify at about 1 to 1½ inches thick. Cut into rectangles or triangles, brush with olive oil, and grill or fry for a couple of minutes on either side until golden brown.

For soft polenta, stir in the Parmesan and the butter just before removing from the heat and season generously. Serve immediately on warmed plates.

GRILLED POLENTA *with* CHOPPED OLIVES *and* ANCHOVIES

For 4, as a snack

Olives are one of those miraculous ingredients that have the ability to transform. Throw a few olives onto a pizza or toss a handful into a salad and the game is instantly raised. In this preparation, with the addition of anchovies and capers, two equally brackish bedfellows, the whole ensemble tickles the tongue in a particularly thrilling way.

I prefer to make this chunky and rustic, so I steer clear of the food processor, but if you like yours smoother, more like the classic Provençal tapenade, whiz away until it's fine and spreadable.

10½ ounces black olives, pitted
4 anchovy fillets, chopped
2 tablespoons capers, finely chopped
½ a clove of garlic, very finely chopped
the juice of ½ a lemon
a small handful of basil leaves, shredded
flaky sea salt
freshly ground black pepper
extra virgin olive oil
4 × ½-inch-thick slabs of grilled polenta (see page 171)

Place the olives in a pile on a large chopping board and, using a very large, wide-bladed knife, chop as finely as you can, in both directions across the board, back and forth several times. Transfer to a large mixing bowl with the chopped anchovies, capers, garlic, lemon juice, and shredded basil. Stir to fully incorporate, adding a good pinch of salt and a twist of black pepper.

Continuing to stir with one hand, slowly add olive oil with the other in a steady drizzle until the mixture resembles a thick paste.

Dollop generously onto the grilled polenta.

GRILLED POLENTA *with* WILL MUSHROOMS *and* GARLIC

For 4, as a snack

One of the great year-round pleasures of visiting the fruit and vegetable markets of Venice is seeing the changing variety of mushrooms on sale. The morels of spring and the girolles of summer are just as appealing as those dark, robust porcini that are so abundant in the autumn. Whatever the weather, this dish works with any fungus you can get your hands on. Remember, when cooking mushrooms, you should never wash them. They absorb water like sponges and you'll just end up with a puddle in the pan and a severely diluted flavor. Dust them off with your hands or a soft brush. And don't chop them up too much—I think it is so much nicer to see the shape of the mushroom in the finished dish.

1 pound wild mushrooms
extra virgin olive oil
1 clove of garlic, finely chopped
flaky sea salt
freshly ground black pepper
a handful of flat parsley leaves, roughly chopped
4 × ½-inch-thick rectangles of grilled polenta (see page 171)

Carefully slice the mushrooms or, if they are small and delicate, leave them mostly intact. Heat a splash of olive oil in a large, heavy-bottomed frying pan and gently sauté the garlic for about a minute without letting it turn brown. Add the mushrooms, a very good pinch of salt, and a twist of black pepper and continue to cook for about 5 minutes, until the mushrooms are softened somewhat and uniformly glossy. Add the chopped parsley, a little more salt if necessary, and sauté for a further minute.

Lay the grilled polenta, now at room temperature, on four plates and distribute the mushrooms equally, finishing with a final flourish of freshly ground black pepper.

WHIPPED SMOKED MACKEREL
on GRILLED POLENTA

For 4, as a snack

I am a fan of the shortcut, particularly if the results are tasty and quality is not compromised. For this reason, I find those prepackaged, vacuum-sealed smoked mackerel fillets very handy when I'm in a hurry. I'm fond of my smoked mackerel panzanella (see page 86) and will make it several times during the warm months, when tomatoes are excellent. This preparation, however, softens the mackerel in texture and flavor, making it perfect as a topping for a slab of grilled polenta. The addition of horseradish gives the whole ensemble a little kick. This also works wonderfully well with crisp carta di musica crackers from the deli and pickled cucumber (see page 170).

2 smoked mackerel fillets, skin removed
1 cup crème fraîche
the zest and juice of 1 lemon
2 teaspoons freshly grated horseradish
flaky sea salt
freshly ground black pepper
4 × ½-inch-thick rectangles of grilled polenta (see page 171)

Place the mackerel on a chopping board and, using two forks, pull the flesh in opposite directions to create rustic, stringy flakes. Put into a large mixing bowl, add the crème fraîche, lemon juice, and horseradish and combine roughly. Season with salt and pepper, turn the mixture once more, and serve on the rectangles of grilled polenta. Scatter the lemon zest over evenly.

Alternatively, divide between four small bowls and place on large plates, with a few pieces of *carta di musica* and a generous amount of pickled cucumber.

WET POLENTA *with* BROWN SHRIMP

For 6

There are certain ingredients that are only available in Venice, often because they are specific to the unique environment of the lagoon or indigenous to the land on the islands within it. Schie are an example. These are tiny shrimp, usually fried and eaten whole. They have a gloriously fishy, nutty flavor. Thankfully, there is an alternative for Italophile home cooks in the US. Brown shrimp have a similar nutty taste and work extremely well with the smooth, lavalike polenta.

1 × soft polenta (see page 171)
¼ cup (½ stick) butter
½ pound cooked brown shrimp or small shrimp
flaky sea salt
freshly ground black pepper

Put the butter into a large frying pan over medium heat until it has melted. Add the shrimp with a good pinch of salt. Sauté for about 3 minutes, until they take on a darker, golden brown hue.

Use a tablespoon to scatter the sautéed shrimp over the polenta evenly, and finish with a light twist of black pepper.

PAN-FRIED SEA TROUT, *and* SALICORNIA *with* LEMON BUTTER

For 4

Friuli-Venezia Giulia, the region just to the northeast of Veneto, is one of the most beautiful and surprising parts of Italy. Its proximity to Austria and Slovenia gives it a decidedly alpine personality at the borders, while on the coastal threshold of the Adriatic, dominated by the capital, Trieste, there is a strong fishing tradition and a distinctive local cuisine. Sea trout is a popular fish there, usually served with a piquant green sauce.

Those Friulian fishing boats often make it to Venice and when I find sea trout at the market, I like to cook it simply with salicornia, a firmly textured and salty succulent similar to what we would call samphire, and which I have also heard called finocchio marino—sea fennel. The robust flavor of sea trout is complemented beautifully by this tangy sauce, adding a wonderful creamy acidity. Once again, if you can find Amalfi lemons, all the better.

½ pound salicornia (samphire; asparagus or green beans can be substituted), washed
extra virgin olive oil
flaky sea salt
4 fillets of sea trout
¼ cup (½ stick) salted butter
the zest and juice of 1 Amalfi lemon (about 2–3 tablespoons juice)
freshly ground black pepper

Place a pan of water over high heat and steam the salicornia for about 4 minutes.

Now, put a good glug of olive oil into a hot frying pan. Sprinkle a little salt on both sides of each fillet and place them in the pan skin side down. There should be plenty of hissing and steam. Fry for 90 seconds, so the skin is browned and crisp, then turn over. After 1½ minutes, switch the heat off.

Meanwhile, melt the butter in a small saucepan over medium heat. Add the lemon juice, 1 teaspoon of the zest, and a twist of black pepper, turn the heat up a little, and whisk gently with a fork. Continue to reduce the lemon butter sauce until it takes on a syrupy consistency.

Lay the trout fillets on four warmed plates, skin side up, shake the moisture from the salicornia, and scatter evenly on top. Spoon over the lemon butter sauce, add a further small pinch of black pepper, and serve.

The Doge's Palace and the Fourth Column

St. Mark's Square, often described as Europe's drawing room, is one of the most beautiful architectural open spaces in the world. It is visited by tens of thousands of tourists daily. But Venetians hardly ever set foot in it. The combination of crowds, plastic souvenir stalls, pigeons, and tour groups makes it, for the residents of Venice, one of the most unpleasant experiences in the city.

To be fair, it is not just St. Mark's Square that Venetians avoid. The area around Rialto Bridge can get stiflingly congested, so much so that streets become impassable, and Strada Nova in Cannaregio, particularly in the summer months, resembles a mile-long rugby scrum. It's one of the reasons I choose to live at the Giardini end of Castello—there are no major tourist attractions, the tour groups don't venture much farther east than the Bridge of Sighs, and the streets are mostly empty, even in high season.

But there is a good reason to visit the area in front of St. Mark's Square, known as the *piazzetta*. This apron of Istrian stone has an important historical significance for being the place where convicted criminals and enemies of the Republic were executed. There are two impressive columns; one holding aloft the winged lion of St. Mark; the other supporting St Theodore and a rather sad-looking crocodile. It was between these two markers, in the early sixteenth century, that one of Venice's greatest villains met his death. A sausage maker named Biagio

was caught after the gruesome discovery of a small finger in a bowl of soup made from his *muséto*. He confessed to abducting, murdering, mutilating, and cooking several children who had disappeared in his neighborhood. After being dragged through the city tied to a horse, flaying the serial killer alive, he was publicly tortured, had his hands cut off, was then de-limbed at the shoulder and thigh, and finally beheaded right here between the columns.

However, I sometimes come to this cheerful tourist hotspot for a different column. There are eighteen of them flanking the front of the Doge's Palace at ground level, from the *piazzetta* on the left to the Bridge of Sighs on the right. If you look at the fourth column in from the left, you will notice that it protrudes just a little farther from the front of the palace and that the ledge between column and paving stone is just a little narrower. For centuries, schoolchildren have played the following game: stand with your back hard against the column, and try to move from one side to the other without touching the pavement. It seems like an easy enough challenge but it is, as I have discovered myself on several attempts, impossible. Legend has it that condemned men were given this task as a final chance of salvation. The possibility of freedom and life must have seemed so tantalizingly close, but failure was inevitable. They were all executed anyway.

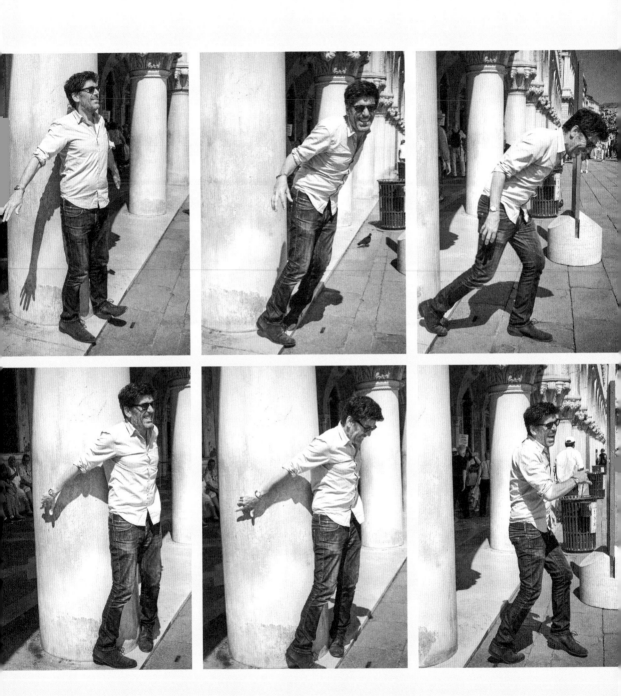

VEAL "QUAIL" KEBABS

For 4, as a starter

This is a country curiosity with origins in the villages and farmsteads of rural Veneto. Quite often, much in the way of medieval feasts, certain meats were made to resemble other beasts. This recipe is known in Italian as quagliette di vitello—"little quails of veal." I wonder whether, in the foothills of the Dolomites, quail was seen as a little more refined and perhaps rarer than garden-variety veal? Whatever the reason, I love to prepare this with little fanfare and explanation. Someone always asks what it is, and then the fun starts.

The great Elizabeth David mentions this in her excellent Italian Food, with a version that uses stale bread, onion and bacon fat. In my experience, the "quails" produce plenty of flavor and moisture on their own.

1½ pounds boneless veal loin
flaky sea salt
freshly ground black pepper
8 small slices of prosciutto
16 large sage leaves
8 thin slices of pancetta
4 × 10-inch wooden skewers, soaked for 15 minutes in cold water
extra virgin olive oil

Cut the veal loin into two flat pieces, then spend some time with a wooden rolling pin and a large chopping board pounding and flattening them even more. Ideally they will each end up around 8 inches square and ¾ inch thick.

Cut each piece into four so that you are left with eight 4-inch squares. Liberally season with flaky salt and freshly ground pepper. Lay a slice of prosciutto on each veal square and fold the edges in. Place 2 sage leaves on each. Preheat the oven to 400°F/200°C.

Now roll up the bundles and carefully wrap the pancetta slices snugly around each. Push 2 bundles onto each of the four moistened skewers and lay them on an oiled baking sheet. Drizzle a little more oil on the bundles.

Place in the oven for 8 to 10 minutes, turning once or twice. Serve hot, on the skewers, wait for the first questions, and then you can start telling your little story.

ROASTED PORK INVOLTINI
with PROSCIUTTO *and* GARLIC

For 4

There is a long tradition in rural Italy of creating stuffed joints of meat by layering ingredients and rolling them into a solid cylinder. Then, by slicing through the joint, the cross-section reveals a delicious spiral of contrasting colors, flavors, and textures. This particular involtini works very well as a roast to put in the middle of the Sunday lunch table with potatoes, or with the individual slices served on their own as a starter with a simple watercress salad.

5 ounces crustless stale bread, finely chopped
whole milk
1½-pound boneless pork loin
6 slices of prosciutto
extra virgin olive oil

4 cloves of garlic, very thinly sliced
flaky sea salt
2 large handfuls of arugula leaves,
   stems removed
freshly ground black pepper

Place the chopped stale bread in a small bowl and pour over enough milk to just cover it. Leave to stand for 10 minutes, until the bread has absorbed most of the milk.

Meanwhile, using a large wooden mallet or a rolling pin, pound and flatten the pork loin to a ¾-inch thickness, then cut into 4 rectangular pieces. Set aside.

Cut the slices of prosciutto into ribbons. Place 8 wooden skewers (or toothpicks) in cold water to soak and preheat the oven to 375°F/190°C.

Warm a good glug of olive oil in a large frying pan over a low to medium heat. Add the garlic and a generous pinch of salt and gently sauté for a few minutes, until the garlic is glossy and translucent. Carefully add the separated prosciutto ribbons, making sure they don't clump, cook for an additional couple of minutes, then add the arugula and the milk-soaked bread, squeezing out the excess milk first. Turn up the heat just a tad, stir for a minute or two to fully incorporate, add a splash of the excess milk if it's looking too dry, then remove from the heat.

Give both sides of the flattened pork a good crunch of salt and a twist of black pepper, then divide the arugula and prosciutto mixture equally between the pork pieces and spread evenly. Roll them up tightly from the long side of the meat and secure each roll with soaked skewers where the seam overlaps, to stop them unfurling. Place on an oiled baking sheet with a drizzle of olive oil and roast for 15 minutes.

Rest for 5 minutes, then remove the skewers and, using a very sharp knife, slice each roll three times at even intervals to create 4 little *involtini* per person.

STUFFED ROAST PORK ROLL (PORCHETTA)

For 8

There is such a pleasurable sense of ceremony when bringing the roasted porchetta out of the oven and to the table that guests cannot help but be caught up in the occasion. The cooking aromas that fill the kitchen while the meat is roasting only fuel the anticipation and make the meal feel more like a feast.

It is an absolute family favorite in homes across northern Italy and a dish by which you should not be daunted. The ingredients are very easy to come by, most butchers are more than happy to prepare and trim the pork belly, and the method, once you've got the hang of the trussing part, is fairly straightforward. Rest the joint before slicing and use a very sharp knife. The skin turns beautifully crisp after nearly three hours in the oven, and precise, clean slices will show off the beautiful cross-section swirl of stuffing.

extra virgin olive oil
1 large onion, finely chopped
½ pound chicken livers, cleaned and chopped
flaky sea salt
8 to 8½ pounds boneless pork belly, excess fat
  trimmed
freshly ground black pepper

6 cloves of garlic, finely chopped
a large handful of sage leaves, chopped
a large handful of rosemary leaves,
  chopped
fronds from 2 large fennel bulbs, chopped
2 teaspoons fennel seeds
a small glass of red wine

Heat a good glug of olive oil in a saucepan and gently sauté the onion for 5 minutes, until soft and glossy. Add the chicken livers and a good pinch of salt and continue to cook until nicely browned and incorporated with the onion. Remove from the heat and allow to cool.

Preheat the oven to 400°F/240°C. Lay the pork belly on a large board, skin side down, and apply a generous quantity of salt and freshly ground black pepper. Massage well with your hands and allow to rest for 5 minutes.

Now spread the chicken liver mixture evenly over the surface of the pork belly. Evenly distribute the chopped garlic, sage, rosemary, and fennel fronds over the top. Finally, scatter over the fennel seeds and drizzle with a little olive oil. Carefully roll the meat into a cylinder, then, using eight 12-inch pieces of string, tie the joint securely, making sure the filling stays put. Push it back in if it oozes out.

Place the pork in a roasting pan, smother with salt, pepper, and a few glugs of olive oil, and massage with your hands. Put it into the oven for about 20 minutes, turning it once or twice until nicely browned, then reduce the oven to 300°F/140°C and roast for 2½ hours.

Remove the pork from the oven, transfer to a large wooden chopping board, and cover with foil. Allow to rest for 15 minutes. Meanwhile, put the roasting pan directly on the stovetop and heat the meat juices, scraping the juicy bits that have stuck to the bottom and adding a splash or two of red wine. Reduce until slightly syrupy and remove from the heat.

Slice the porchetta into ¾-inch-thick portions and serve with a spoonful or two of the reduced meat juices. This goes particularly well with cooked green lentils mixed with gently fried *soffritto* (see page 303).

LITTLE CABBAGE BUNDLES

For 4

It is unlikely that you will find this delightful dish on many restaurant menus, but it is very popular in the homes of northern Italy. Originally from Lombardy, it reminds me of rissoles or traditional meaty bundles, but these are given a much more attractive twist with the use of cabbage leaves instead of sheep's caul. The dish was described to me by Mrs. Scarpa, who lives in a ground-floor house near the altar to the Madonna in Corte de Ca'Sarasina. She didn't have a name for it, but when I suggested I might call it fagotti di cavolo (thinking this meant "cabbage bundles") she looked confused. Fagotti is Italian for bassoons. No wonder the locals think me odd.

1 large Savoy cabbage
1 ounce stale bread, chopped into small pieces
whole milk
½ pound ground veal
a large handful of grated Parmesan
1 medium egg
1 large spicy pork sausage
flaky sea salt

freshly ground black pepper
grated nutmeg
1 leek, to make string
1 clove of garlic, crushed
extra virgin olive oil
a large knob of butter
⅓ cup chicken stock (see page 304)

Cut the core of the cabbage so that the outer leaves fall off. Discard these coarser, dark green leaves, and peel off the more tender, inner ones. Remove any tough, thick stalks but keep the leaves intact. Wash them and put them into a large pan of boiling water for 2 to 3 minutes. Drain them, gently rinse under a cold tap for a minute, then set aside to air dry.

Put the chopped stale bread into a bowl and cover with milk. Leave to soak for about 20 minutes, squashing and stirring occasionally.

Put the veal, Parmesan, and egg into a large mixing bowl. Split the sausage lengthwise with a sharp knife and push the sausage meat out into the bowl, discarding the skin. Add a good pinch of salt and a large twist of black pepper. Using your hands or a wooden spoon, combine well. Add a few gratings of nutmeg, then add the mushy, milky bread, squeezing any excess milk out first. Turn everything over several times to fully combine and incorporate.

Preheat the oven to 350°F/180°C and, meanwhile, cut the leek lengthwise into long strips to create thin ribbons, which you will use as string.

Retrieve the cooled cabbage leaves, scoop a heaped tablespoon of the meat stuffing into the center of each, and roll them up into balls. Tie each parcel with a length of leek string.

Put the crushed garlic and a good splash of olive oil into a large ovenproof dish and coat the entire base and sides. Carefully place the bundles side by side in the dish, put a small dollop of butter on each, pour over the chicken stock, and cover with foil.

Place in the oven for 15 minutes, then remove the foil and bake for a further 15 minutes. Serve the bundles immediately, either on their own or, if you prefer, with a large pot of buttery mashed potato in the middle of the table.

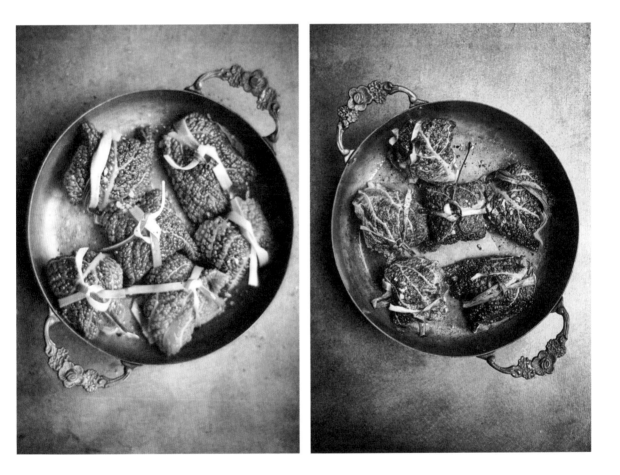

FRIED MEATBALLS

For 4, as a bar snack

In the Cannaregio district of the city, just off Strada Nova, there is an ancient osteria listed in guidebooks as Ca' d'Oro but known locally as Alla Vedova—"The Widow's Place." It is rather charming, particularly in its evocation of nineteenth-century Venice, principally because nothing much has changed for nearly 130 years: What you see really is what you get, and what you have got since 1891.

But while the tables in the two small rooms are popular with tourists, the locals always stand at the bar and order an ombra (a tiny glass of wine) and a meatball. It is the meatballs at Alla Vedova that keep me coming back; they are consistently and unfailingly delicious. The rate with which they are ordered and eaten means there is a constant supply coming from the kitchen, all day long, and they are always hot. I have tried to persuade Mirella, the current proprietor, to share the recipe but she keeps it a closely guarded secret. This, after years of painstaking research and literally hundreds of tastings, is my version.

1 pound ground veal
3 medium eggs
1 cup grated Parmesan
1 clove of garlic, very finely chopped
2 tablespoons plain flour
a small handful of very finely chopped flat parsley leaves

2¾ cups breadcrumbs (1 cup soaked in a little milk, 1¾ cups for coating)
fine salt
ground white pepper
extra virgin olive oil, if needed
vegetable oil

Put the veal, eggs, Parmesan, garlic, and flour into a very large mixing bowl. Using a fork, work all the ingredients together. Now add the chopped parsley leaves, the milk-soaked breadcrumbs, squeezed of excess liquid, a good pinch of salt, and a good sprinkle of white pepper. Mix thoroughly. Cover the mixing bowl and leave to stand for about an hour to let the flavors develop.

Shape the mixture into small balls, adding more breadcrumbs if it is too moist or a little olive oil if it is too dry.

When formed, roll the balls in the remaining breadcrumbs to coat them fully.

In a large, deep-sided frying pan, heat about 1½ inches of vegetable oil until it is hot enough to turn a small piece of bread golden brown in about a minute. Add the meatballs to the hot oil and fry, turning frequently, until they are crispy and golden all around—about 3 to 4 minutes.

Remove with tongs and drain on several sheets of paper towel. Serve immediately, while hot.

MEATBALL SPIEDINI *with* SAGE

For 4

The butcher's shop on Seco Marina, just around the corner, is popular in the mornings. There is often a crowd outside—customers leaning on their wheelie baskets and getting and dishing out the latest local news and scandal. But if I go off-peak, say around noon, I sometimes get to see something you don't witness earlier—meat being minced to order. I know it's a small thing, but it pleases me to know my meat is fresh, and there's something quite satisfying about the way the flesh is squeezed out of the mincer.

These little kebabs are a real hit with my children, and I have even enlisted their help in the mixing part of the recipe. Fun to make and to eat.

3½ ounces stale bread, no crusts, finely chopped
whole milk
7 ounces ground beef
7 ounces ground pork
1 medium egg, beaten
1 clove of garlic, very finely chopped

3½ ounces Parmesan, grated
flaky sea salt
freshly ground black pepper
4 × 10-inch wooden skewers, soaked for 15 minutes in cold water
8 large sage leaves
extra virgin olive oil

Put the stale breadcrumbs into a small bowl and cover with milk. Leave for 20 minutes, turning once or twice with a fork, until the milk has been absorbed and the bread is mushy.

Place the ground beef and pork in a large mixing bowl and add the egg, garlic, and two-thirds of the Parmesan. Turn several times with your hands and add a good pinch of salt and a twist of black pepper. Squeeze the excess milk from the mushy bread and incorporate with the meat mixture, using your hands to achieve a smooth consistency. I find this particularly pleasurable and sometimes go into a bit of a meatball mix trance.

Preheat the oven to 350°F/180°C. Roll the meat mixture into 12 even balls. Push 3 meatballs onto each skewer, with a sage leaf in between. Drizzle a little oil in a baking pan and roll the meatball skewers in it to coat; add salt and pepper and place in the oven for 12 to 15 minutes, turning once halfway through, until golden brown.

Serve with the remaining Parmesan and a hunk of ciabatta.

LITTLE "LOST BIRD" KEBABS

For 4

Along with a handful of other idiosyncrasies, Venetians are particularly playful when it comes to describing food. They will often use a doppelgänger ingredient to name a dish, presenting the traveler or food tourist with curious anomalies.

In Italy in general, small, fried rice balls are "little oranges'" (*arancini*), splayed anchovy fillets are "tongues" (*alici allinguate*), and monkfish is "toad's tail" (*coda di rospo*). Two of the most curious fake recipes are veal "quails" (see page 184) and these "lost birds."

The story behind these traditional country kebabs is almost as tasty as the dish itself. Hunters who were either ineffective or unlucky daren't go back home empty-handed, so would stop by the butcher for whatever scraps he had left. The hunter's excuse would be that he'd lost the birds he'd shot, so this was dinner instead.

The skewers can be loaded with any strong-flavored meats, although I particularly like this combination, served with a simply dressed salad of crunchy red chicory.

9 ounces boneless pork or veal
9 ounces boneless lamb
9 ounces calves' liver
3½ ounces pancetta
8 × 10-inch wooden skewers, soaked for
*   15 minutes in cold water*
a large handful of sage leaves
flaky sea salt
freshly ground black pepper
extra virgin olive oil

With a very sharp knife, cut the pork or veal into 16 large cubes. Do the same with the lamb and liver. Cut the pancetta into 16 smaller cubes. Push 2 of each of the meat chunks, mixed up and alternating, with a sage leaf after every cube, onto the skewers. Add salt, pepper, and a drizzle of olive oil, and grill on a medium-hot barbecue for 6 to 8 minutes, turning frequently. Alternatively, grill on a very hot, oiled grill pan over high heat, or simply roast in a preheated oven at 350°F/180°C for 10 to 12 minutes, turning once. Much better on the barbecue though.

ROASTED SQUASH *with* TOASTED SEEDS *and* SAGE

For 4

When nature, or the greengrocer, offers up great ingredients, it means you have to make less of an effort in the kitchen. As I am fond of saying, good Italian cooking is synonymous with good shopping.

An autumn stroll to Via Garibaldi got me more excited than usual one morning because the color of the vegetable barge had shifted slightly from the previous day, from green to orange. Yes, the squash had arrived.

All you need to do is soften them with heat and highlight their natural flavor with a few herbs and condiments, and nature takes care of the rest. Delicious on their own or with a raw radicchio salad.

1 butternut squash	*chile flakes*
1 acorn squash	*ground cinnamon*
extra virgin olive oil	*freshly ground black pepper*
flaky sea salt	*a handful of sage leaves*

Preheat the oven to 350°F/180°C. Remove and discard the hard stalks from the squash, cut the squash in half, and scoop out the seeds and set aside, discarding any stringy, pulpy bits from the seed cavity. You may need to wash and thoroughly dry the seeds. Peel away any hard, tough bits of skin but retain some areas where the skin is fine and delicate. Cut the squash into bite-size pieces.

Pour a few generous glugs of olive oil into a large roasting pan. Add the squash pieces, a good pinch of salt, a teaspoon of chile flakes, a scant teaspoon of cinnamon, and a good twist of black pepper. Roughly chop half the sage leaves and toss those in along with the remaining whole leaves. Use your hands to toss everything several times, making sure the squash is well coated. Cover tightly with foil and place in the oven. After 20 minutes or so, remove the foil, turn the oven up to 400°F/200°C and roast for an additional 12 to 15 minutes, until the squash is soft but golden and the edges are crisp.

While the squash is roasting, warm a frying pan over medium to high heat, add a splash of olive oil, and gently fry the retained seeds, shaking or stirring to turn frequently, until they have started to puff up slightly and turn golden brown.

Scatter the toasted seeds over the roasted squash and serve.

VENETIAN POTATOES

Enough for 4 to 6, as an accompaniment

What makes these potatoes Venetian is simply the frequency with which I have seen them prepared in this manner in the homes of Giardini. The shape of the cut potatoes sometimes varies (thick disks are quite popular) but I much prefer the dice shape. The consistent features are the melted onions and the unctuous syrupy stock sauce. I wouldn't worry too much about the type of potato, either. With waxy varieties, the dice holds its shape much better and the slightly yellow hue is a little more attractive. But floury spuds disintegrate a tad more, so the sauce has more viscosity, giving a fuller, deeper flavor. I love them both ways.

3 ¼ pounds potatoes
2 large onions
¼ cup (½ stick) butter
extra virgin olive oil
up to 1 ½ cups hot vegetable stock (see page 304)
flaky sea salt
a handful of flat parsley leaves, chopped
freshly ground black pepper

Peel the potatoes, rinse them in cold water, dice them (literally the size of dice), then rest them on a kitchen towel to dry.

Peel and halve the onions, and slice into thin, crescent-shaped slivers. In a large, heavy-bottomed frying pan, melt the butter over medium heat. Add a good glug of olive oil and gently sauté the onions for about 10 minutes, until soft, glossy, and translucent. Put the potatoes into the pan, coat with the oil and onions, and continue to sauté for an additional few minutes.

Now add a couple of ladles of the hot stock and a good pinch of salt. Continue to simmer gently for 3 to 4 minutes. If necessary, add another ladleful of the stock to just cover the potatoes. If the stock is bubbling too fiercely, reduce the heat and simmer gently for about 30 minutes.

When the stock has reduced to a syrupy consistency and the potatoes are soft to the bite, but not disintegrating, add the parsley and a little more salt, if necessary. Serve immediately, while hot, with a generous twist of black pepper.

OVEN-DRIED TOMATOES

Makes plenty—enough to make risotto for 6 or pizza for 4

At the start of the summer, around early May, the markets begin to stock Sicilian tomatoes. These varieties are tasty enough and work well in all tomato dishes, but I somehow feel like it's cheating. It is only when the local tomatoes of true summer arrive, those grown on Sant'Erasmo, for example, that I get excited. The season is long, late May to September, and it seems like a crime to do anything other than eat them raw, cut once or twice, with excellent olive oil and sea salt. (English tomatoes in July and August give me a similar thrill.)

In autumn, I allow myself to start cooking them and preserving a few for winter months (this dish freezes well). It's a great way to impart more depth of flavor and still make them delectable.

20 medium tomatoes
2 teaspoons superfine sugar
2 teaspoons flaky sea salt
a handful of picked thyme leaves

Preheat the oven to 250°F/120°C. Using a sharp, serrated knife, remove and discard the top of each tomato. Place them carefully in a large roasting pan lined with parchment paper and evenly distribute over the sugar, salt, and thyme leaves.

Roast in the oven for about 2½ hours. Allow the tomatoes to cool. If you are using them for tomato risotto (see page 260), remove and discard the skins (they will slip off rather easily). They will keep in the fridge for a week or so.

SWEET *and* SOUR ROASTED ONIONS

For 4

Pickled onions always remind me of English picnics, Boxing Day cold lunches, and the large jars full of them on the counters of fish and chip shops. It is not a sophisticated association. This Venetian preparation is much more subtle. It is the roasting process that makes the difference, allowing the natural sugars to develop and rendering the onions tender and sweet, with just enough of the residual tartness from the vinegar to narrow the eyes ever so slightly.

These are wonderful as an accompaniment to a lunch of cold cuts, cheeses, and bread.

⅓ cup (¾ stick) butter
2¼ pounds small onions, peeled
superfine sugar
2 cups red wine vinegar
a good handful of pine nuts
a good handful of raisins or sultanas
flaky sea salt

Preheat the oven to 325°F/160°C.

Heat the butter in a very large lidded frying pan. Place the onions in the pan in a single layer. Use a second pan or cook in batches if your pan isn't large enough. Sprinkle 4 or 5 tablespoons of sugar over the onions, turn a few times, then add half the vinegar. Cover and cook over a low heat for about 5 minutes, then remove the lid, carefully turn the onions over, and continue to simmer for another 5 minutes, until the liquid has reduced by half.

Transfer the onions to a large ovenproof casserole dish. Add the pine nuts and raisins, a pinch or two of salt, and the remaining vinegar, and cook in the oven for 30 to 40 minutes.

Remove, allow to cool, and serve warm or at room temperature.

GIBSON

For 1

Much has been written about Harry's Bar in Venice, a rather legendary watering hole and something of an institution since it first opened its doors in 1931. It is so eye-wateringly expensive that no sane person would dine or drink there unless for a special treat. I will sometimes take a seat at the bar on those rare occasions when I am visited by friends who know its reputation and are curious to try it.

The most famous drink at Harry's Bar is the Bellini, a combination of white peach purée and prosecco, invented on the premises decades ago. But my tipple of choice is the Gibson. The white-coated bartenders serve it in a very particular way, and this recipe is my approximation of the Harry's Bar Gibson.

2½ ounces very good gin
a few drops of dry vermouth
10 or so small silverskin cocktail onions, drained

Begin by putting the bottle of gin and the glass into which you will serve the cocktail (a small antique tumbler would be my choice) into the freezer for at least half an hour.

Remove the glass and introduce the vermouth. A few drops really is all that is required, a scant ½ teaspoon. Take 2 of the onions and skewer them on a cocktail stick, then place in the glass. Take the gin from the freezer—it should have developed a gloopy, syrupy consistency—and pour about 2½ ounces into the frozen glass. Serve with the remaining onions in a pretty little dish on the side.

OLIVE OIL CAKE

For 8

It may seem counterintuitive to bake a cake using an ingredient so firmly associated with savory dishes, but olive oil cake is an everyday classic that feels distinctly Italian. It's a delicious alternative to butter-based cakes and has a rather grown-up flavor profile, but this will change dramatically depending on the type of olive oil that you use. It goes without saying that you should use the best quality olive oil you can get, but grassy, peppery oils don't lend themselves very well to this cake. Look for an oil that has floral, herby, or fruity notes instead.

Because it is made with oil rather than butter, this cake keeps nicely moist for a good few days. If you want to reanimate it, however, the glaze for the lemon polenta cake on page 212 works very well as a pick-me-up poured on top.

1⅓ cups extra virgin olive oil
1⅓ cups superfine sugar
4 large eggs
½ teaspoon fine salt
1 teaspoon vanilla extract

1 cup whole milk
the zest and juice of 1 lemon
the zest and juice of 1 orange
2 teaspoons baking powder
2¾ cups "00" flour

Use a little of the olive oil to grease a 9-inch cake pan and line the bottom with parchment paper. Preheat the oven to 350°F/180°C.

Put the sugar, eggs, salt, and vanilla extract into a large mixing bowl and beat until pale and fluffy. Using a wooden spoon, slowly stir in the olive oil, milk, and lemon and orange juice. Add the two zests. In a separate bowl, mix the baking powder into the flour, and when combined, fold into the olive oil mixture until smooth.

Pour the cake mix into the greased pan and bake for about 45 minutes, until the top feels springy, a skewer comes out clean when inserted into the middle, and the cake is golden brown.

Cool on a wire rack and serve warm, generous slices with a sweet wine, or enjoy cold the next day with coffee.

LEMON POLENTA CAKE

For 8

Here's a really popular cake that is easy to make and both traditional and controversial at the same time. The traditional part is that it is made with almonds and polenta rather than flour, therefore good for those trying to avoid gluten. The controversial bit is that I have borrowed the syrup from that perennial English vicar's tea party favorite, lemon drizzle cake, albeit with superior fruits from Amalfi.

4 Amalfi lemons
1⅓ cups superfine sugar
¾ cup (1½ sticks) butter, very soft
1 teaspoon vanilla extract
fine salt
1 teaspoon baking powder
6 medium eggs
1 cup polenta
1½ cups ground almonds

Start by zesting the lemons and set the zest aside. Now juice them, removing any pits.

Grease a 9-inch springform cake pan and preheat the oven to 350°F/180°C.

Put two-thirds of the sugar and all the butter into a very large mixing bowl and beat together with a wooden spoon until pale and creamy. Add the vanilla extract, a pinch of salt, the baking powder, half the lemon juice and zest, and then, beating all the while, add the eggs, one at a time, and fully incorporate.

After a minute of beating together, slowly fold in the polenta and the ground almonds, mix together well, and spoon the mixture into the cake pan.

Bake for 45 minutes or so, until golden brown. You can test for doneness by inserting a metal skewer into the center—it should come out clean. Remove the cake and place on a wire rack to cool for half an hour.

While the cake is cooling, make the syrup by putting the remaining superfine sugar into a medium saucepan with the remaining lemon zest and juice and about ⅓ cup of water. Bring to the boil while stirring, reduce for a few minutes until syrupy, then take off the heat.

Serve slices of the warm cake with the syrup and perhaps a dollop of mascarpone cream, or enjoy later at room temperature with a coffee.

FRIED CUSTARD

For 6

I was served this dessert at a farmhouse near Conegliano, just where the Dolomite mountains begin. I don't have a particularly sweet tooth and, in any case, I was rather full from an excellent supper of grilled shellfish and a seafood risotto. But my host, a winemaker, was gently insistent and I am far too well-mannered to appear ungrateful, so I tucked in. What a treat. The set custard starts to turn soft again inside the breaded crust when it is fried, so the first bite releases a delicious, sweet ooze. Make sure your timing is right—they are perfectly pleasant when cold, too liquid when hot, but completely delicious when warm.

6 medium eggs
1 cup superfine sugar
1½ cups "00" flour
3⅓ cups whole milk

the zest of 1 lemon
2 cups vegetable oil
2 cups panko breadcrumbs
confectioners' sugar

Separate the eggs into two bowls, one large, one medium—yolks in the large one, whites in the other. Whisk the yolks with a fork. Lightly whisk the whites and set aside. Pour the superfine sugar into the large bowl with the yolks and mix together. Using a fine sieve, very slowly whisk in the sifted flour. Now, whisking steadily and firmly with one hand and pouring evenly with the other, slowly add the milk, ensuring that there are no lumps and that the mixture is smooth and custardy.

Place the custard in a medium saucepan with the lemon zest and, over a low heat, stirring steadily the whole time, bring the mixture to a gentle bubble. It will thicken to a consistency more like honey or treacle, at which point remove from the heat.

Line a wide, shallow pan with parchment paper and evenly pour in the custard to a thickness of ¾ inch to 1½ inches. Leave to cool.

Once the custard has set, cut into small rectangles the size of business cards. Put about a ½ inch depth of vegetable oil into a large, deep frying pan and place over high heat until it reaches 375°F/180°C. You can test this by putting a small cube of white bread into the oil—the bread should turn golden within 20 seconds or so.

Dip the rectangles of set custard into the lightly whisked egg whites and then into the panko breadcrumbs until they are coated on all sides. Fry each one in the oil for 45 seconds or so, until golden brown. You may need to do this in batches and you may need to replenish the oil. Remove and rest on paper towel to drain.

While they are cooling, dust the rectangles with confectioners' sugar and serve while still slightly warm, or later at room temperature.

PISTACHIO LOAF

For 8

Baking is as popular in Venice as it is anywhere. Home cooks always seem to have a cake at the ready. The activity of baking is somehow separate from cooking the family meal, however, and there are certain recipes that appear more suited to an afternoon indulgence rather than the dinner table. The shape of this dessert is a dead giveaway, having the perfect dimensions for slicing a treat to go with a coffee.

The small handful of whole shelled pistachios adds a really lovely texture and looks great in cross section when the loaf is sliced, but make sure they're not too coarse.

a small handful of whole,
  shelled pistachios
1½ cups superfine sugar
the seeds from 1 vanilla pod
the zest of 1 lemon
1½ cups (3 sticks) butter, very soft

6 medium eggs
fine salt
1¼ cups ground almonds
1¼ cups ground pistachios
1¼ cups "00" flour
1 teaspoon baking powder

Grease a large loaf pan. Preheat the oven to 350°F/180°C.

Put the whole pistachios into a mortar and pound roughly for a minute with a pestle. Set aside.

Put the sugar into a very large mixing bowl and add the vanilla seeds and the lemon zest. Stir with a wooden spoon, add the butter, and beat for a few minutes until the mixture is pale and fluffy.

Now add the eggs, one at a time, and beat them into the sugar and butter until well incorporated. Add a pinch of salt and then fold in the ground almonds and pistachios. Finally, slowly add the flour and baking powder, stir thoroughly until the mixture is smooth and battery, mix in the reserved pounded pistachios, and pour into the greased loaf pan.

Bake on the middle shelf of the oven for 45 to 50 minutes, until golden brown and a metal skewer comes out clean if pushed into the center.

Turn the loaf out of the pan and rest on a cake rack to cool for about 20 minutes. Slice and eat warm with an espresso or a glass of sweet wine.

WARM RADICCHIO, PANCETTA, AND CHICKPEA SALAD • LENTIL AND LEEK BRUSCHETTA WITH SOFT-FRIED EGG • CREAMED SALT COD CROSTINI • CREAMED STOCKFISH FROM VICENZA • TUNA MEATBALLS • VENETIAN PASTA AND BEAN SOUP • BREAD SOUP (PANADA) • CACIO E PEPE • PIZZOCCHERI WITH CAVOLO NERO AND POTATOES • CHICKEN LIVER TAGLIATELLE • DUCK RIGATONI • RABBIT PAPPARDELLE • LINGUINE CARBONARA • WILD BOAR RAVIOLI • TAGLIATELLE SECOE • MEATBALL PIZZA • TOMATO RISOTTO • TARDIVO AND VERY GOOD RED WINE RISOTTO • CHESTNUT AND WILD MUSHROOM RISOTTO • CHICKEN CACCIATORE • PORK IN MILK • PORK RIBS WITH CABBAGE • SALTIMBOCCA • SLOW-ROASTED VEAL SHIN • VEAL CHOPS WITH SAGE AND LEMON • ROAST LEG OF LAMB WITH ANCHOVY AND ROSEMARY • CASTRADINA • BAKED STUFFED ONIONS • GRILLED RADICCHIO • VENETIAN MANHATTAN • ESPRESSO AND SAMBUCA GRANITA • FRITOLE (VENETIAN DOUGHNUTS) • VENETIAN RICE PUDDING POTS

WINTER

"Abhorrent, green, slippery city."

D. H. Lawrence

✳

In the winter months of November, December, and January, I am acutely aware that Venice is a city built on water. The lagoon and the canals are a presence year-round, of course, but it is when the cold winds blow from the Dolomite mountains in the north and the chilly tides of the Adriatic push in from the south and east that water occupies a more prominent position in my consciousness.

Water is everywhere. The 177 canals are a permanent reminder of that. In the *campi* you will usually find a fountain, too, pumping drinking water all day long. The direct connection to the lagoon makes the two largest waterways, the Guidecca Canal and the Grand Canal, appear more like the sea, with visible tidal movement and choppy waves. And then there is Acqua Alta . . .

Acqua Alta (High Water) is the expression Venetians use to describe the winter phenomenon of a tide breaching parts of the city and flooding the squares and streets. The higher the tide, the more severe the floods, and the greater the chance of water entering homes, shops, businesses, and hotels. It is, naturally, extremely distressing for residents but something they have become used to. There is a warning system that sounds several hours before the high tide arrives—an air-raid siren followed by a series of high-pitched beeps that indicate the height of the tide. Additionally, elevated walkways are placed in those

winter

parts of the city worst affected. Everyone puts on galoshes or, if it is a particularly bad one, rubber boots. Furniture is moved to upper floors.

Acqua Alta can be exacerbated by heavy rain and strong winds. Rain has a strange effect on Venice even at the best of times. In severe downpours, it can feel oppressive. In a city built of stone and marble, the rain has nowhere to go and moisture levels tip over the edge. The expression "soaked to the bone" takes on an almost literal meaning—it really can feel like your bones are getting wet. In the period after a rainstorm, the slightly softened sounds of trolleys on bridges and vaporetti chugging along are actually quite pleasant, but it can take a long time to feel dry again.

On November 4, 1966 Venice suffered Acqua Alta of catastrophic proportions. The combination of two high tides, three days of rain, a powerful easterly wind, and swollen mainland rivers discharging into the lagoon meant that parts of the city were submerged to a depth of around shoulder height for twenty-four hours.

Winter also brings bright days, when the air is cold and crisp and the skies wide and blue. Winter light seems sharper, the low angle of the sun means it bounces off pale terracotta walls and floods squares and courtyards with a bright, pink glow. The reflection of the sun on the lagoon creates a remarkable sheen with a milky shimmer. It is on days like these that the elders of the city, rather than stay indoors sheltering from the harsh winter temperatures, come out in force, usually draped in their most impressive fur coats. With the addition of hats, scarves, gloves, and sunglasses, it's impossible to tell who is who. When it's icy, or when it has snowed, it is not uncommon to see my neighbors walking arm-in-arm, men with women, women with women, and men with men. (In fact, Venice is the only city I know where it is quite normal to see elderly men walking arm-in-arm no matter what the weather, a practice I intend to adopt in my dotage.)

The nights are a different matter. Venice sleeps early year-round—by 9 or 10 p.m. everything is either closed or winding down—but in winter, the city goes to bed even earlier. Venice is the old lady of Europe. Walking the deserted streets at night, however, is something I rather enjoy. The sound of water lapping against the sides of the canals and the echo of footsteps on the hard paving stones have a dreamlike quality. The city's street lighting is so low it tends to drain away all the colors, and Venice transforms into a black and white version of itself.

Early winter mornings bring another delight. Because the waters of the canals and lagoon are a mere few inches beneath the stone paving slabs of the streets, squares, and promenades, Venice gets its very own sea mist. This tends to hover at knee height until it dissipates as the day progresses, but while it lasts it is a beautiful special effect, worthy of any Hollywood horror movie.

The city is so much quieter in winter. I will often walk to Rialto Market on a fine morning in order to treat myself to produce I can't get locally, and the normally packed streets will be blissfully empty. I take the *traghetto* from Strada Nova across the Grand Canal to the market. (A *traghetto* is a manually oared ferry used by locals to cut out the long distances required on foot if you stick to the four bridges of Rialto, Accademia, Scalzi, and Contituzione.) There are six crossing points on the Grand Canal and these are sometimes referred to as the "invisible" bridges. As you step in, the oarsman offers his forearm, which you take, and you pay a few coins for the ninety-second journey. There seems to be only one unwritten rule: ladies may sit, gentlemen should stand. The *traghetti* are decommissioned gondolas, no frills, no gold, always black (by city decree), no soft furnishings, and quite often a bit bruised and battered.

Rialto Market in November and December is a treat. The feast of Maria della Salute on November 21 is an important date in the Venetian calendar and most of the city gears up for that by buying a castrated lamb, but at other times the fish stalls and vegetable stands here are as welcoming as any market I know. Much of the greengrocery—hearty cavolo nero and intense purple radicchio—comes from the mainland, from the farms and fields of Veneto. Winter is the time of the year when Venice connects most fully with the forests and mountains of northern Italy and the two cuisines find a meeting place.

It is this time of the year that the markets are easily navigable, too, and locals don't have to put up with tourists, photographers, and tour groups. With my Venetian trolley and a shopping list, I fit in quite neatly and enjoy feeling like a local myself.

WARM RADICCHIO, PANCETTA, *and* CHICKPEA SALAD

For 4

In winter, my culinary default setting is roasts, stews, brassicas, and meats. The icy mountain winds and chilly ocean tides turn Venice into a fridge, and a particularly cold one at that.

Occasionally, however, the sun will rise on a gloriously clear day and, despite those freezing temperatures, it will actually feel slightly warm to the cheeks. This, combined with a big blue sky and Venice's bright, milky white light, sets me thinking about food that is delicate, not heavy; textured, not soft.

I'm a fan of warm winter salads in general and this one in particular, since it does the great courtesy of hitting the agrodolce nail on the head: bitterness from the radicchio and sweetness from the pancetta. The reserved cooking juices at the end are very important—they give the salad a subtle warmth and help to very slightly wilt the radicchio leaves.

1 cup dried chickpeas
1 bay leaf
2 heads of Treviso tardivo radicchio
extra virgin olive oil
8 ounces pancetta, cubed

a small handful of flat parsley leaves,
  roughly chopped
1 small red onion, very finely sliced
red wine vinegar
freshly ground black pepper
flaky sea salt

Soak the chickpeas overnight, then drain and rinse. Transfer to a pot of boiling salted water with a single bay leaf and gently cook for about 45 minutes, until tender. Drain and set aside, discarding the bay leaf.

Remove and discard the core of the radicchio and slice the leaves lengthwise into thin strips. Wash in clean cold water and drain thoroughly using a salad spinner. Place in a very large mixing bowl and set aside.

Heat a couple of teaspoons of olive oil in a large, heavy-bottomed frying pan and add the pancetta cubes. Cook over medium heat for about 5 minutes, until crispy and golden brown. Using a slotted spoon, remove the pancetta and place on paper towels. Reserve the cooking fat.

Now add the drained chickpeas, parsley, sliced red onion, and pancetta to the mixing bowl, with a good glug of olive oil, a tablespoon of vinegar, and a tablespoon of the reserved cooking fat, and gently mix together using your hand, taking care not to crease or crush the radicchio leaves. Add a good twist of pepper and a couple of pinches of salt, turn once more, and serve on four large plates.

LENTIL *and* LEEK BRUSCHETTA *with* SOFT-FRIED EGG

For 4

Lentils are traditionally eaten on New Year's Eve with cotechino sausage because they are seen as a symbol of good fortune for the approaching twelve months. The round shapes of the individual pulses resemble coins.

In Italy, New Year's Eve is rather an abstemious event (unlike in the United States). A few glasses of wine may be drunk, of course, but the emphasis is on food rather than booze. This brunchy dish is a perfect post-midnight snack to see in the new year, enjoy some lucky lentils, and ward off the January 1 hangover.

¼ cup (½ stick) butter
2 large leeks, washed, trimmed,
    and very thinly sliced
flaky sea salt
¾ cup plus 2 tablespoons red wine
1⅓ cups dried green or Puy lentils

3 cups hot water
red wine vinegar
extra virgin olive oil
4 very large free-range eggs
4 good thick slices of sourdough, toasted
freshly ground black pepper

In a large frying pan, melt the butter over medium heat and sauté the leeks until soft and translucent, about 4 minutes. Add a few pinches of salt. Increase the heat a little, add the wine, and simmer for about 8 minutes, until most of it has bubbled away.

Add the lentils to the pan and coat them thoroughly with the leeks and reduced wine. Pour in the hot water, cover, reduce the heat to medium-low, and simmer for about 20 minutes, until the water is absorbed. (Check the instructions on the lentil packet—times can vary depending on the brand.) Take off the heat, add a splash of red wine vinegar and a good glug of olive oil, stir once or twice, cover again, and set aside.

Heat 2 tablespoons of olive oil in a nonstick frying pan over medium heat. Carefully crack the eggs into the pan and fry until the whites are firm but the yolks are still shiny and runny. You may need to do this in batches.

Place the toasted sourdough on four separate plates, divide the lentil mix equally among the slices, and gently transfer the eggs from the pan to sit on top of the lentils. Finish with a final pinch of salt and a few twists of black pepper.

CREAMED SALT COD CROSTINI

For 4

It is not possible to write about Venetian cuisine without mentioning baccalà mantecato, also known as creamed salt cod. This delicate, fluffy confection is such an intrinsic part of the culinary identity of the city that you will find it everywhere, in restaurants, bàcari, wine bars, delicatessens, supermarkets, and homes, and in myriad manifestations.

Traditional preparation can sometimes be elaborate, but this version is surprisingly easy and still delivers delicious and authentic results. If you find it difficult to come across pre-soaked salt cod, simply buy dried salt cod and soak it for twenty-four hours in cold water, changing the water three or four times. The flesh flakes away from the carcass quite satisfyingly.

10½ ounces boned, soaked salt cod
1 bay leaf
1 clove of garlic, peeled and halved
the juice of 1 lemon
a very small palmful of finely
*   chopped flat parsley leaves*

flaky sea salt
freshly ground black pepper
extra virgin olive oil
1 small baguette

Place the salt cod in a large saucepan and add enough cold water to cover all the flesh. Drop in the bay leaf and the garlic and bring to a boil. Pour in the lemon juice, reduce to a bubbling simmer, and cook for half an hour or so, stirring from time to time. Drain the cod, retaining a cupful of the cooking liquor, and remember to fish out and discard the garlic and bay leaf.

Put the cod pieces into a large mixing bowl with the chopped parsley, a few pinches of salt, and a good twist of black pepper. Using a wooden spoon, stir enthusiastically while pouring in a steady, thin stream of olive oil to create a smooth and stiff paste. This part of the process, the *mantecatura*, requires quite a bit of elbow grease in order to achieve the characteristic fluffy consistency. Use the retained cooking liquid to loosen the mixture if necessary, but it needs to be stiff enough to form peaks when manipulated. Taste the *baccalà* at this stage and add more salt and pepper if necessary.

Slice the baguette at an angle into elliptical disks, toast them, then generously dollop the creamy cod onto each, finishing with a flourish of olive oil.

CREAMED STOCKFISH *from* VICENZA

For 4

This dish, baccalà alla vicentina, is often eclipsed by its more famous cousin baccalà mantecato. Whereas the latter is made from salt cod, soaked, whipped, and infused with garlic, the former uses stockfish, which is air-dried rather than salted, and has the addition of a soffritto and anchovies. It really is a labor of love and takes a few days of preparation, but if I have guests and I really want to impress, it is certainly worth the effort. I have to say I also get a little sense of achievement, too. But don't worry—despite being time-consuming, it is relatively easy and the results are delicious. (By the way, you may be surprised at the inclusion of Parmesan in the ingredients list. This is one of those rare occasions when cheese combined with fish is acceptable. It is a practice that is normally frowned upon in Italy but, according to Francesco at the excellent restaurant Antiche Carampane, a peculiarly Venetian phenomenon.)

1 large dried stockfish, about 1 pound
extra virgin olive oil
10½ ounces soffritto (see page 303)
flaky sea salt
1 ounce anchovies

a handful of flat parsley leaves,
roughly chopped "00" flour
3 ounces Parmesan, grated
freshly ground black pepper
1 ½ cups whole milk, maybe more

Two to three days before making this dish, you need to soak the dried stockfish in fresh, cold water, changing it twice a day. After the last rinse, drain, then break the flesh into a large mixing bowl, discarding the bones.

Take a large, lidded cast-iron casserole dish, heat 3 or 4 tablespoons of olive oil, and gently sauté one-third of the *soffritto* with a very good pinch of salt, for about 5 minutes, until soft and glossy, but not browned. Now add the anchovies, parsley, and 2 or 3 tablespoons of flour, and continue to sauté and stir until the anchovies have melted and the paste is thick and glossy.

Add half the flaked stockfish to the pan and spoon over another third of the *soffritto*. Add half the Parmesan and a twist of black pepper. Put the remaining stockfish on top of this, the last of the *soffritto*, and then a final scattering of Parmesan and a twist of pepper. Pour in the milk (and a little more if necessary) to cover everything, place over low to medium heat, and simmer, covered, for about 2 hours, until all the milk is absorbed and the stockfish is soft. During this period, stir very occasionally, only to stop the mixture sticking to the bottom of the pan.

Serve hot, with soft polenta (see page 171), and keep the remainder in the fridge to serve at room temperature with crusty bread over the next few days.

TUNA MEATBALLS

Makes 10 to 12 balls

Over the years, as I have eaten my way around Venice, I have occasionally become fixated on a particular dish and, in the absence of documented instructions (or, indeed, simply the confidence to ask), I have set about literally dissecting the thing with a fork where I sit, or with my hands where I stand. So it was with the tuna meatballs at Al Merca, the spritz bar near Rialto Market. They are frustratingly tasty little squashed spheres, served cold, and I was determined to re-create them in my kitchen.

After a few goes, I came up with this and, even though I say so myself, I'm pleased with the result. The tuna is tangy and firm, the potato adds a lovely softness, and the garlic is just a note, not too strong. You can enjoy them warm, straight from the fryer, or at room temperature like they are at Al Merca.

2 medium potatoes, yukon gold red
¼ cup (½ stick) butter
½ a clove of garlic, very finely chopped
flaky sea salt
ground white pepper
1 ½ cups canned tuna (drained weight)

a small handful of flat parsley leaves,
*   finely chopped*
ground cinnamon
extra virgin olive oil
6 cups vegetable oil, for deep-frying
1 ¼ cups instant polenta

Peel the potatoes, quarter them, and put them, into a large pot of boiling water for 12 to 15 minutes, until well cooked but not falling apart. Drain them thoroughly and set aside for 10 minutes to cool a little.

When the steam is starting to subside, mash the potatoes in a very large mixing bowl with the butter, garlic, a good pinch of salt, and white pepper. If you have a ricer, pass them through that a few times. Now add the drained tuna, the chopped parsley, and a pinch of cinnamon. Mix all the ingredients together very well into a smooth but stiff paste, loosening with a little olive oil if too dry. Taste and adjust the seasoning with salt and white pepper if necessary. Roll into even balls, about the same size as ping pong balls, then flatten a little.

Heat the oil to just under 400°F/200°C in a large pan. Test by dropping a cube of bread into the oil. It should turn golden brown in under 30 seconds.

Put the polenta on a large shallow plate and roll each ball in it generously to coat completely. Using a slotted spoon, lower the tuna meatballs carefully into the hot oil and fry for 1½ to 2 minutes, until golden brown. Remove and rest on paper towels, to drain, and serve as snacks with a spritz.

VENETIAN PASTA *and* BEAN SOUP

For 4

There are some dishes that provide the sort of comfort you need when recovering from flu or heartache. Pasta and bean soup is not sophisticated and certainly doesn't require a great deal of skill to prepare, but its healing qualities are second to none and I find a large bowl on a cold night is all the soothing I need. It's a family favorite all over Italy, but what makes this version particularly Venetian is the absence of tomatoes. In Tuscany, it'd be red and saucy (also delicious in its own way), but in Veneto the conversion of half the broth to purée makes for a flavor and texture that takes me straight back to the nursery.

1 cup dried borlotti beans, soaked overnight in cold water
extra virgin olive oil
1 clove of garlic, chopped
3½ ounces unsmoked pancetta, cubed
7 ounces soffritto (see page 303)

2 teaspoons chopped rosemary, no stalks
8½ cups hot chicken stock (see page 304)
1½ cups ditalini (or short macaroni)
flaky sea salt
freshly ground black pepper
grated Parmesan, to serve

Drain and rinse the borlotti beans. Heat 2 tablespoons of olive oil in a large saucepan for which you have a lid. Gently sauté the chopped garlic and the pancetta for a couple of minutes, until the meat is starting to color. Add the *soffritto* and a splash more olive oil. Coat every part of the *soffritto* and sweat for 10 minutes or so, until glossy and soft.

Add the drained beans and the chopped rosemary, turn over a few times, then add the chicken stock. Bring to a boil, then reduce to a low simmer, cover with the lid, and leave for 2 hours, until the beans are tender.

Using a slotted spoon, remove about half the beans and purée them in a blender. Once they have a smooth consistency, return them to the soup, then add the pasta and a little more water if necessary, a good pinch of salt, and a twist of black pepper. Cook for an additional 10 minutes, adjust the seasoning, and serve in warmed bowls. Scatter over the Parmesan and drizzle a little olive oil on top of each serving, and make sure you have plenty of crusty bread on hand.

BREAD SOUP (PANADA)

For 4 to 6

This is peasant food, pure and simple. The Italian tradition of cucina povera is well known in rural areas but manifests itself in Venice, too, and panada is probably the best example. It uses the most basic ingredients, stale bread, but is as lovingly prepared as if it were expensive, exotic, or refined. It is the philosophy of making the most of what is available that appeals to me in dishes such as this.

Panada was a favorite Venetian dish of the poet Percy Bysshe Shelley, a vegetarian, and is traditionally finished with a crucifix-shaped drizzle of olive oil.

extra virgin olive oil
a large knob of butter
2 cloves of garlic, peeled and finely chopped
12½ ounces stale bread
grated nutmeg
freshly ground black pepper
flaky sea salt
6⅓ cups vegetable or chicken stock (see page 304)
7 ounces Parmesan, grated

Heat a good glug of olive oil and the knob of butter in a large saucepan and gently sauté the garlic, making sure it does not brown. After a minute, crumble the stale bread into the pan and coat with the oil, butter, and garlic. Add a few gratings of nutmeg, a couple of good twists of black pepper, a decent pinch of salt, then the stock.

Turn the heat up and bring very briefly to a boil, then reduce to a low simmer. Cover with a lid at an angle to leave a small opening and allow to gently bubble away for about 45 minutes.

When the soup has reduced in quantity by about one-third, ladle into warmed bowls, equally scatter the Parmesan, and carefully drizzle over a little olive oil to create a crucifix on the surface of each serving.

CACIO E PEPE

For 4

This Roman impostor is very popular in Venice and has had something of a revival in London and New York of late, too. I can understand why—it's the perfect dish. There are two principal ingredients and they work together to create something that is greater than the sum of their parts.

In Cannaregio, near the Ghetto, there is a restaurant called Paradiso Perduto. It's a loud and brash place, always packed with students, artists, bohemians, poets, musicians, and (ahem) philosophers. The proprietor, Maurizio, is a charming eccentric with a scant regard for authority. He usually only closes his restaurant at night when the police come and tell him to. But the homemade pasta is excellent and the cacio e pepe is an event. An entire wheel of Pecorino is brought to the table on a trolley and the hot pasta turned within it. If you get a chance to visit, I highly recommend it.

This recipe does take a bit of practice and if you are not fast enough or your pasta not hot enough, the cheese may clump. Don't despair, try it again and once you have the hang of it, you won't look back. It is such a comforting classic that it really is worth the effort.

a handful of black peppercorns
1 pound dried tonnarelli or spaghetti

a large knob of good butter
3¾ cups finely grated Pecorino Romano

First, put the black peppercorns into a small frying pan over a high heat. Dry-fry them for 2 minutes, shaking the pan frequently. Set aside until they are cool, then put into a mortar and pound with the pestle until roughly ground.

Bring a large pot of salted water to a boil and cook the pasta according to the package instructions. When the pasta is al dente, drain, but retain the cooking water and leave it on a medium heat. Set the drained pasta aside.

Now, speed is of the essence. In a separate large, heavy-bottomed pot, melt the butter over a medium heat and scatter in most of the grated Pecorino, stirring quickly with a wooden spoon. Still stirring, use a ladle to add a little of the cooking water to the pot. Keep the spoon going, adding more cooking water if necessary to create a smooth, glossy sauce. Add the drained pasta and continue to stir until every strand is coated, adding a little more cooking water if the sauce looks too stiff (but be careful not to make it too watery).

Serve immediately on four warmed plates and scatter a generous amount of the toasted ground peppercorns and the rest of the Pecorino onto the mounds of steaming cheesy pasta.

PIZZOCCHERI *with* CAVOLO NERO *and* POTATOES

For 4

Buckwheat pasta is, if anything, more of an authentic preparation than the conventional durum wheat variety made with strong, fine "00" flour. There is a lovely rustic texture to buckwheat and the pasta behaves differently once cooked, with a little more firmness and less viscosity. Pizzoccheri is an ancient recipe, dating back many centuries, generally thought to originate in the mountainous region of northern Lombardy but popular in rural parts of Veneto, too.

As a winter dish, I'd say it is pretty perfect, both warming and satisfyingly starchy. The Asiago, if aged, will crumble satisfyingly, a little like Parmesan, but if the cheese is young, you should slice it thinly and lay it over the hot pasta and potatoes to allow it to melt before stirring.

For the pasta:
1⅔ cups buckwheat flour
⅔ cups "00" flour, plus extra for dusting
fine salt
2 large egg yolks, beaten

For the sauce:
1 large potato, peeled and diced
1 large head of cavolo nero, stalks
   removed, leaves cut lengthwise

⅓ cup (¾ stick) butter
1 clove of garlic, finely chopped
a small handful of sage leaves,
    cut lengthwise
flaky sea salt
freshly ground black pepper
7 ounces Asiago, crumbled or sliced
   (see above)
3½ ounces Parmesan, grated, for serving

Make the pasta: Mix the two flours together in a large bowl with a good pinch of fine salt. Tip on to a clean work surface and make a mound with a deep well in the middle. Tip the egg yolks into the well and, using a fork, gradually bring the flour, little by little, into the center, adding 1 or 2 tablespoons of cold water to create a firm dough. Knead the dough for around 10 minutes, until smooth and springy, then form it into a ball and cover, resting it for about half an hour. Clean and dry the work surface and liberally dust with flour. Turn the dough out and, using a floured rolling pin, roll out to the thickness of a coin. Cut into long strips, about ½ inch in width, and set them aside.

Make the sauce: Bring a large pot of salted water to a boil and drop in the potatoes. After 2 minutes, add the cavolo nero. Stir, and after an additional 2 minutes add the pasta. Stir again and, after a final 2 minutes, turn the heat off, wait 30 seconds, then drain. Set aside briefly.

Simultaneously, over a medium heat, melt the butter in a very large, deep frying pan. Sauté the garlic and sage leaves for 2 minutes. Now add the drained pasta, cavolo nero, and potatoes, a good pinch of flaky salt and a twist or two of black pepper. Reduce the heat to low, and carefully turn everything over a few times with tongs. Add the Asiago and remove from the heat. Gently turn all the ingredients one more time, incorporating the pasta with the sauce, and divide equally among four warmed plates. Serve with the Parmesan in a bowl for scattering at the table.

CHICKEN LIVER TAGLIATELLE

For 4

Choices are often influenced by budget and it is the economy cuts and bargains that naturally appeal to the person in charge of the household purse. Additionally, there is often an inverse relationship between expense and flavor. The more costly options at the butcher—fillet steaks and chicken breasts—are not nearly as flavorsome as their cheaper counterparts—beef rib and chicken thighs. This is certainly true of chicken livers, too: in the bargain basement of offal but in the penthouse for flavor.

When I bought chicken livers at my local butcher on Seco Marina, two things made me smile: the weight of the meat was (as is always the case) slightly more than I had asked for but for the same price, and the livers were wrapped in newspaper. Old school.

10½ ounces chicken livers
flaky sea salt
freshly ground black pepper
1 pound dried tagliatelle
a scant ½ chicken stock cube

extra virgin olive oil
⅓ cup butter (¾ stick)
a small handful of sage leaves
2¾ ounces Parmesan, grated

Clean the chicken livers in cold running water, removing the blood clots and fatty membranes. Lay on paper towels and pat dry. Roughly chop the livers and season with a few pinches of salt and a twist of black pepper. Set aside.

Bring a large pot of salted water to a boil and cook the tagliatelle according to the package instructions. Reserve a cupful of the pasta cooking water and dissolve the crumbled stock cube into it. Drain the tagliatelle when it is just al dente.

Meanwhile, heat a good glug of olive oil with half the butter in a large, heavy-bottomed frying pan and, over medium heat, sauté the livers and sage leaves until browned. Add the drained tagliatelle to the frying pan and mix the livers and sage to incorporate with the strands of pasta. Turn the heat up a little higher and add the cup of reserved chicken stock–pasta water. Stir well for 1 minute more, then remove from the heat. Add the remaining butter and most of the grated Parmesan, turn over a few times in the pan to make sure the butter is melted, and serve on warmed plates. Sprinkle the remaining Parmesan as a final flourish at the table.

DUCK RIGATONI

For 4

Every once in a while I will come across a sauce that is so successful and so tasty that I tend to make it at every opportunity. This one started when the butcher began displaying duck legs at a very reasonable price and I felt compelled to buy a few without much of an idea what to do with them. It turned out duck ragù is locally traditional and, after a few tweaks, this recipe produced a most effective sauce. As with many Venetian meat dishes, the addition of cinnamon gives it a distinctive regional accent.

extra virgin olive oil
4 duck legs
2 large onions, finely chopped
1 large carrot, finely chopped
1 large celery stalk, finely chopped
1 clove of garlic, crushed
flaky sea salt
freshly ground black pepper
1 tablespoon ground cinnamon
"00" flour

a glass of red wine
1 ¼ cups passata (tomato purée)
1 × 14-ounce can diced or chopped
*   tomatoes*
1 bay leaf
a small handful of picked thyme leaves
1 cup chicken stock (see page 304)
whole milk
1 pound dried rigatoni
3 ½ ounces Parmesan, grated

Take a large, lidded ovenproof saucepan. Heat a good glug of olive oil over a medium heat and fry the duck legs, turning frequently, until brown on all sides, about 10 minutes. Remove from the pan and set aside.

Add another glug of olive oil to the pan and preheat the oven to 300°F/150°C. Sauté the onions, carrot, and celery for around 10 minutes, until soft and glossy. Add the garlic and stir for a further minute. Return the duck legs to the pan, add a good pinch or two of salt, a few twists of black pepper, the cinnamon, and a handful of flour and stir. Pour in the wine, allow to bubble for a few minutes, then add the passata, the tomatoes, the bay leaf, and the thyme. Pour in the stock and turn the heat up a little. When the liquid boils, turn off the heat, cover the pan with the lid, and place in the oven. Leave for 2 hours, stirring just once, halfway through.

Remove the pan from the oven, locate the duck legs, and carefully lift them out. Discard the fat and bones, shred the meat with a knife and fork, and put the flesh back into the pan. Add a splash of milk and put on a low to medium heat to simmer gently.

Bring a large pot of salted water to a boil and cook the rigatoni according to the package instructions. When done, reserve a cup of the cooking water and drain the pasta. Add the pasta to the duck sauce, stir to coat completely, loosening with a little of the reserved pasta water if it seems too dry. Finally, stir in the Parmesan and serve.

RABBIT PAPPARDELLE

For 4

Across the Liberty Bridge, the two-and-a-half-mile-long umbilical cord that connects Venice to the mainland (which many proud Venetians would like to see demolished, by the way), there is a vast area that comes under the political and municipal jurisdiction of the greater region of Venice. It includes the coastal industrial towns of Marghera and Mestre, but also the rural pastures and farmsteads beyond. The easiest meat to come by in this part of Italy has always been rabbit, and it is deservedly prominent in traditional Venetian cooking.

I love rabbit, particularly the gamey wild variety, and it is well suited to rich sauces such as this one here. Rabbit meat has a delicacy that is absent in cultivated livestock, and those who tell you it tastes like chicken are missing the point.

extra virgin olive oil
1 whole rabbit, jointed
    (the butcher will do this)
1 large onion, finely chopped
1 medium leek, washed, trimmed
    and finely sliced
1 large carrot, finely chopped
3 ounces pancetta, finely cubed
2 cloves of garlic, very finely chopped
1 tablespoon passata (tomato purée)
a small handful of rosemary, chopped,
    no stalks

a small handful of thyme, chopped, no stalks
a small handful of sage leaves, chopped
flaky sea salt
freshly ground black pepper
a glass of white wine
2¼ cups chicken stock (see page 304)
1 pound dried pappardelle
Dijon mustard
ground cinnamon
4¼ ounces Parmesan, grated
a large knob of butter

Heat a couple of glugs of olive oil in a large, heavy-bottomed pot for which you have a lid, and sear the rabbit pieces on all sides so that they are golden brown. Set aside.

Add another glug of olive oil to the same pot and return to the stovetop, reducing the heat to low. Add the onion, leek, carrot and pancetta and sauté gently for around 10 minutes, until the onion is soft and translucent and the pancetta is starting to get crispy. Return the rabbit to the pot with the garlic, passata, and herbs and stir for a minute, with a good pinch of salt and a few twists of black pepper. Pour in the wine. Stir. Add the stock. Stir. Cover the pot with the lid, reduce the heat to low, and leave to simmer gently for about an hour and a half.

The rabbit will be incredibly tender, so very carefully remove the pieces and place them on a chopping board. Using a knife and fork, separate the flesh from the bone. Discard all the bone, gristle, fat, and pinbones, shred the meat, and set it aside.

Meanwhile, cook the pappardelle in a large pot of boiling, salted water for 2 minutes less than the package suggests. Bring the heat up fully on the other pan for about 4 to 6 minutes, until the liquid has reduced by half. Return the shredded rabbit to the sauce, reduce the heat to low, then add a heaping teaspoon of mustard and a level teaspoon of cinnamon. Add the drained pasta and stir well for 2 minutes to coat every strand of the pappardelle and incorporate the sauce fully. Fold in most of the Parmesan and all the butter. Remove from the heat. Taste and add a little more salt and pepper if needed.

Now, using pasta tongs, carefully divide the incorporated pasta and sauce among four warmed plates and finish each with a scattering of the remaining Parmesan.

LINGUINE CARBONARA

For 4

This classic causes more controversy than any other Italian dish. There is never such a thing as a definitive recipe, since all regions will have their own variations (Rome is its real home), but I have seen so many chefs, cooks, and food writers get hot under the collar about carbonara that I thought twice about including my version in this book.

Having said that, I have steered away from scandal by keeping things conventional. I use egg yolks rather than eggs, for a richer, more golden sauce, and I use a little Pecorino along with the Parmesan to create a bit of a tang. Guanciale, the fatty pork cheek, is great if you can get it, but good pancetta is fine if not. But, dear reader, under no circumstances should you use cream. It is just wrong.

1 pound dried linguine
5¼ ounce chunk of pancetta (or, even better, guanciale),
    cut into thick, short matchsticks
freshly ground black pepper
4 large free-range egg yolks, beaten
¼ cup (½ stick) cold butter, cut into small cubes
3½ ounces Parmesan, grated
¾ ounces Pecorino, grated

Bring a large pot of salted water to a boil and cook the linguine according to the package instructions.

Meanwhile, heat a large, heavy-bottomed frying pan. When it is very hot, add the pancetta and sauté until it is starting to crisp and is turning golden brown. (No need for oil, the pancetta will release its own oil and fry nicely.)

Just before the linguine is done, scoop out 2 cupfuls of the cooking water and set aside. Drain the pasta when al dente and transfer to the pan of pancetta. While still over very low heat, coat every strand of linguine with the oil that has been released from the pancetta and make sure it is well incorporated. Add a few good twists of black pepper, too.

Now, remove the pasta and pancetta from the heat, add the beaten egg yolks, the butter cubes, and the Parmesan, and stir vigorously with a cup of the retained cooking water. Continue until the glossy sauce coats all the pasta strands. Add more pasta cooking water from the second cup if necessary.

Divide equally among four warmed plates. Add the grated Pecorino and a few more generous twists of black pepper.

WILD BOAR RAVIOLI

For 4

Perfection is overrated. The most pleasing and attractive people and things tend to have small quirks and blemishes. I always prefer to eat as a guest in someone's home than in a restaurant, for example, and the sometimes clumsy way of the home cook is much more appealing to me than the precision of a professional chef.

When I am making ravioli, I use an old French pâtissier's rolling pin and a wonky pasta cutter. The resulting shapes are uneven but I wouldn't want them any other way. I suggest you don't try to be too precise when cutting your pasta, either. Additionally, when stuffing the parcels, there is no need to be neat. A rustic aesthetic suits this unctuous ravioli and will remind you and your guests that nobody's perfect.

extra virgin olive oil
1 large onion, peeled and finely chopped
1 large carrot, peeled and finely chopped
1 large celery stalk, peeled and
  finely chopped
1 clove of garlic, peeled and finely chopped
1 pound wild boar shoulder, trimmed
¾ cup plain flour, seasoned with fine salt
3 ounces pancetta, cubed

1 teaspoon ground cinnamon
passata (tomato purée)
a glass of red wine
a small handful of oregano leaves
1 × fresh pasta for ravioli (see page 302)
flaky sea salt
4¼ ounces Parmesan, grated
a large knob of butter
freshly ground black pepper

Heat a very good splash of olive oil in a large, lidded, heavy ovenproof casserole dish over medium heat. Gently sauté the onion, carrot, celery, and garlic so that the mixture becomes glossy and translucent, about 10 minutes.

Meanwhile, cut the wild boar into cubes and dust lightly with the seasoned flour. In a separate frying pan, heat a glug of olive oil and brown the pieces of boar all over. You will need to do this in batches, replenishing the oil when necessary. Set aside. Preheat the oven to 325°F/160°C.

Put the pancetta into the casserole dish with the vegetables and cook for 3 to 4 minutes, until it has started to release its fat. Now add the browned boar and the cinnamon and stir. Mix in about 2 tablespoons of the passata. Pour the glass of wine into the frying pan that contained the meat, bring to a bubble, scrape the sticky burnt bits off the bottom of the pan, and pour into the casserole. Add the oregano, fill the wine glass with water, and pour that in, too.

Cover the casserole dish with the lid and place in the oven for about 1½ hours. Check once or twice to make sure it isn't drying out. When done, the meat will have disintegrated and the sauce reduced to a sticky syrup. Use a wooden spoon to break up the larger pieces, then set aside to rest.

Roll the pasta out into a large thin sheet, dusting with a little flour if necessary. Using a pastry cutter, cut 3-inch squares. When the wild boar *ragù* has cooled sufficiently, place a generous teaspoonful on each of the squares. You may need to squeeze some of the liquid from the *ragù* if it is too wet. Fold over the pasta like a small envelope, sealing with your fingers and edging with the tines of a fork. Set the ravioli aside.

Bring a large pot of salted water to a boil, carefully lower in the ravioli, cook on a gentle boil for 3 to 4 minutes, then remove, drain and transfer to a large, warmed serving dish. Carefully fold in the grated Parmesan and the butter, and finish with a few twists of black pepper.

TAGLIATELLE SECOE

For 4

At the western tip of Venice, where the Cannaregio Canal joins the lagoon, you'll see a very impressive building on the left, just past the famous "Three Arches" bridge. Although now part of the Foscari University, it was once the city's abattoir and, for a cuisine famed for its seafood, meat was once big in Venice.

Several feet away on the same fondamenta, there is a little trattoria called Dalla Marisa. It is an unassuming canteen, frequented by local tradespeople, residents, and the occasional tourist, and the menu is short and inflexible; you get what you are given. The reason it is popular is that the cooking is traditional, authentic, and delicious, just like mamma used to make.

Marisa still occasionally cooks there, but it's mostly her daughter at the stove. One of my favorite dishes is spaghetti secoe. Traditionally made with fatty nuggets of meat picked from the spinal column of the cow, it is subtly flavored with cinnamon and doesn't have the soupy consistency of some meat sauces. It's a lovely connection with history and a flavorsome alternative to that more famous ragù from Bologna.

extra virgin olive oil
a knob of butter
4 large tablespoons soffritto (see page 303)
10½ ounces ground minced fatty beef or
    veal
a small glass of red wine
2 tablespoons passata (tomato purée)

flaky sea salt
freshly ground black pepper
ground cinnamon
1 pound fresh tagliatelle (or dried if you
    prefer)
4¼ ounces Parmesan, grated

Heat a good few glugs of olive oil and the butter in a large pan. Gently sauté the *soffritto* on a medium heat for 10 minutes, until translucent and glossy. Add the ground meat and stir until it has broken up and is nicely browned. Add the wine and when it has evaporated, turn down the heat to low and add the passata and a good pinch of salt and pepper. Now, carefully scatter 2 good teaspoons of ground cinnamon evenly over the sauce and stir. Make sure the heat is as low as possible, then cover and simmer for around 45 minutes, stirring occasionally.

Toward the end of the sauce's cooking time, place the fresh tagliatelle in a large pot of salted boiling water and cook for 3 to 4 minutes (or cook dried tagliatelle according to the package instructions). Drain, reserving a cup of the pasta cooking water, and add the tagliatelle to the pan of sauce. Mix together well. Use a little of the pasta cooking water to loosen the sauce, but only if necessary. Stir in the Parmesan and serve.

MEATBALL PIZZA

For 1

Like most people living in and around Corte de Ca'Sarasina, there are times when I just can't be bothered to cook. And on those occasions, I feel like going to the Madonna in the al-fresco altar at the bottom of the street and offering thanks that we have a local pizza restaurant that does takeout.

Dai Tosi (see also page 60) is a community service as well as an excellent pizzeria. I spent two weeks in winter living off their takeouts and not much else. And on many occasions I have tried to emulate their pizzas at home. For this one, I set myself the challenge of using ingredients solely bought from the local co-op (the butcher was closed) and I was rather happy with the result. A lot depends on the quality of the sausage, so do get the best.

a satsuma-size ball of pizza dough
 (see page 301)
plain flour, for dusting
2 tablespoons tomato sauce (see page 300)
2 hot Italian sausages
extra virgin olive oil
½ a ball of buffalo mozzarella

½ a clove of garlic
dried oregano
chile flakes
a small handful of grated Parmesan
flaky sea salt
freshly ground black pepper

Stretch, flatten, and roll the dough on a floured surface until it is a rough disk of around 9 inches or so. Try to leave the edges a little thicker and the shape uneven. Place it on a lightly oiled baking sheet.

Using the back of a large spoon, spread the tomato sauce evenly over the pizza base, stopping ½ inch from the edge. Preheat the oven as high as it will go.

Using a sharp knife, slice the sausages lengthwise, push out the meat, and discard the skins. Shape the sausage meat into about 8 or 9 small balls. Heat a glug of olive oil in a frying pan and gently fry the balls until golden brown. Carefully place them on the pizza base and break up and distribute over the mozzarella, too. Slice the garlic as thinly as you can and scatter it over the surface with a pinch of oregano and as many chile flakes as you can handle.

Place the baking sheet directly on the top shelf of the oven, closing the door quickly. Bake for around 6 minutes, but do keep an eye on it and remove it when the edges are starting to turn dark brown and the cheese is bubbling. Remove and immediately scatter the Parmesan over the surface, with a drizzle of olive oil, a pinch of salt, and a twist of black pepper.

TOMATO RISOTTO

For 4

I have deliberately included this bright and delicious risotto in the winter chapter because there are times you need a little bit of sunshine on the plate when there is so little coming through the window.

Legitimate fresh tomatoes have long since disappeared from the market stalls by December, but those oven-dried tomatoes you made in the autum and froze (see page 202) will come in very handy now. The roasting process intensifies the flavor of tomatoes, so you will find this risotto wonderfully rich and rounded. The tomato pulp turns the rice pink, too, so the dish brings a little color to the table.

6⅓ cups vegetable stock (see page 304)
⅓ cup (⅔ stick) butter
1 large white onion, very finely chopped
flaky sea salt
1¾ cups Carnaroli rice
a small glass of dry vermouth
10 medium oven-dried tomatoes (see page 202)
4¼ ounces Parmesan, finely grated
freshly ground black pepper

Heat the stock in a large saucepan and keep it simmering with a ladle at hand. Melt half the butter in a large, heavy-bottomed saucepan over medium heat and sauté the onion, with a good pinch of salt, until glossy and translucent, turning frequently with a wooden spoon. Add the rice and ensure each grain is coated.

Pour in the vermouth, and when the liquid has almost all evaporated, reduce the heat to low, add 1 ladle of stock and stir. Repeat this process for about 10 minutes, carefully adding a small ladle of stock at a time, never allowing the rice to fully dry out but not flooding it either. Gently introduce the tomatoes to the pan and incorporate carefully with a wooden spoon. Continue to add a little stock at a time while stirring for another 5 minutes.

When the rice is almost done, but still has a bit of bite (test a grain between your front teeth), add a final splash of stock, the remaining butter, and turn up the heat. Stir for 30 seconds (but try not to bash the tomatoes too much) and remove from the stove. Add most of the Parmesan, stir once or twice, and taste. Adjust the seasoning if necessary. Serve on warm plates, scatter over the remaining Parmesan, and finally garnish with a twist of black pepper.

TARDIVO *and* VERY GOOD RED WINE RISOTTO

For 4

Although I have seen Treviso tardivo (the king of radicchio, its elegant curled fronds resembling an octopus in flight) as early as October, strictly speaking it shouldn't be harvested until much later. Stefano, my favorite greengrocer on Via Garibaldi, is adamant. When I asked for it one November he said, "Impossible." "Why's that?" I asked. "Because we haven't had the first frost. Tardivo means late, and until there is a frost, it can't be picked." You don't argue with Stefano.

2 heads of Treviso tardivo radicchio
6⅓ cups vegetable stock (see page 304)
⅔ cups (1⅓ sticks) butter
1 large white onion, finely chopped
flaky sea salt

1¾ cups Carnaroli rice
a large glass of very good red wine
   (Amarone or Barolo should do it)
5¼ ounces Parmesan, grated
freshly ground black pepper

Cut out the hard stalk of the Treviso tardivo and discard. Remove the finest, most delicate fronds and set aside. Chop the remaining radicchio into bite-size pieces.

Heat the stock in a large pot and once it's boiling, reduce to a gentle simmer. Melt one-third of the butter in a large heavy-bottomed pot and add the chopped onion with a good pinch of salt. Over medium heat, sauté gently for 10 minutes, until the onion is soft and translucent.

Add the rice and turn up the heat a little. Make sure every grain is coated with the melted butter and incorporated with the chopped onion. Add the wine, and enjoy the steamy aroma as it starts to evaporate. Stir with a wooden spoon, add the chopped radicchio and reduce until almost dried out, then add a ladleful of the stock. Turn the heat down and continue to add more stock, a little at a time, so that the risotto is never flooded but never dry either.

After about 15 minutes, test a grain of rice between your teeth. There should be a soft resistance to the bite but not too hard. Add a little more stock if necessary for an additional 2 or 3 minutes. Add the remaining butter and turn the mixture enthusiastically several times with the wooden spoon. At this stage, stir in the reserved delicate radicchio fronds and reduce the heat to its lowest setting, then add most of the grated Parmesan and fold into the risotto. Remove from the heat. Taste and adjust the seasoning if necessary by adding a pinch or two of flaky salt. Stir once or twice more, cover, and rest for 1 minute.

Serve a generous spoonful or two on warmed plates with a twist of black pepper and a scattering of the remaining Parmesan.

CHESTNUT *and* WILD MUSHROOM RISOTTO

For 4

Although there are excellent fresh mushrooms available throughout November and December, I am partial to the dried variety I can pick up in neighborhood delicatessens. In my local alimentari, Ortis (see page 268), they sell dried *marzolini*, also known as mousserons in France and St. George's mushrooms in England. They are amazing and taste even more intense after being dried, then reanimated with warm water. Furthermore, the water in which the mushrooms have soaked lends another hit of umami to the risotto in a way that fresh mushrooms cannot.

I marry the deeply delicious porcini and marzolini here with chestnuts for an unequivocally wintry combination of flavors and textures. You will also notice that I use butter instead of olive oil to sauté the shallots. This is a traditional variation in northern Italy, dating back to the era before the 1950s when olive oil from the south wasn't readily available. Only purists, traditionalists, and very old people cook this way these days, but I really like the creaminess you get with this method.

12 chestnuts
1¾ ounces dried porcini
1¾ ounces dried marzolini (mousserons);
    winter chanterelles can be substituted
6⅓ cups chicken stock (see page 304)
½ cup (1 stick) butter
2 large banana shallots, very finely chopped

flaky sea salt
1¾ cups Carnaroli rice
a glass of dry vermouth
a handful of flat parsley leaves
4¼ ounces Parmesan, grated
freshly ground black pepper

First, preheat the oven to 350°F/180°C. Using a small knife with a very sharp point, score the chestnuts with a single shallow incision from one side to the other. Scatter on a baking tray and roast for 15 to 20 minutes, until starting to brown. Remove and allow to cool before peeling. Break the chestnuts roughly with your hands. Set aside.

While the chestnuts are roasting, soak the dried mushrooms in 2 cups of boiled hot water for about 20 minutes. Drain and retain the soaking water.

Now heat the stock in a large saucepan and bring to a very gentle bubble. Leave simmering with a ladle close by.

Melt half the butter in a large, heavy-bottomed saucepan over medium heat and add the chopped shallots with a few pinches of salt. Sauté until glossy and translucent, turning frequently with a wooden spoon, then add the rice. Make sure every grain is coated.

Pour in the vermouth, inhale the delicious cloud of steam, and when the liquid has nearly evaporated, add 1 ladle of stock and stir. Repeat this for 10 minutes, carefully adding the stock a little at a time, never allowing the rice to dry out but not flooding it either. Carefully add the drained mushrooms and stir once or twice with a wooden spoon. Now add a little of the mushroom soaking water, a bit at a time, for an additional 5 minutes.

When the rice is almost done, but still has a bit of bite (test a grain between your front teeth), add a final splash of stock, the remaining butter, and the chestnuts, and turn up the heat just a little. Add the parsley, very gently stir, cook for a final 2 minutes, then remove from the heat. Sprinkle in most of the Parmesan, turn over once, and cover. Rest for a minute.

Serve in warmed bowls, with a twist of black pepper and the remaining Parmesan scattered over the top.

CHICKEN CACCIATORE

For 4

This dish is well known all over the region, and since it roughly translates as "huntsman's chicken stew" it is easy to imagine the eponymous fellow throwing everything into a single cooking pot after a hard day in the forest. I'm using chicken whereas traditionally this dish would have been made with rabbit, and I marinate the pieces for a deeper flavor, but the real beauty of this dish is that it is a one-pot wonder. There is something wholesome and comforting about the entire dish being placed on the table.

4 skinless free-range chicken thighs,
*   on the bone*
4 skinless chicken legs
flaky sea salt
freshly ground black pepper
2 cloves of garlic, sliced
a bundle of rosemary, thyme, and sage,
*   tied with string*
2 bay leaves

2 large glasses of red wine
plain flour, for dredging
extra virgin olive oil
2 large onions, peeled and sliced
2 celery stalks, chopped
2 large carrots, peeled and chopped
2 × 14-ounce cans of plum tomatoes
a handful of pitted black olives

You need to start preparing the day before you want to cook. Place the chicken pieces in a single layer in a deep-sided container. Add liberal amounts of salt and pepper and one of the sliced garlic cloves. Drop in the bundle of herbs and the bay leaves, and cover with the red wine. Use a wooden spoon to squash and maneuver everything to ensure best coverage. Place in the fridge overnight.

The next day, remove the chicken (but retain the marinade) and shake excess wine from the pieces. Lightly dredge them in flour, heat a few glugs of olive oil in a very large, cast-iron, ovenproof casserole dish for which you have a lid, and brown the chicken all over. Set the chicken aside. Reduce the heat to medium, add another good splash of olive oil, and sauté the onions for 5 minutes, until starting to brown. At this point, preheat the oven to 300°F/150°C.

Add the second sliced garlic clove, the celery, and the carrots, and stir. Crunch in a few pinches of salt flakes and a good couple of twists of black pepper. After 5 more minutes, add the chicken pieces with the tomatoes, olives, and finally the reserved red wine marinade with an extra wineglass full of water. Stir a few more times, take off the stove, place a lid on, and put into the oven for about 2 hours, stirring once halfway through.

Before serving, remove the bay leaves and the bundle of herbs. I like to place the entire casserole in the center of the table on a terracotta tile, with a ladle, a stack of bowls, some tumblers, and a bottle of Valpolicella.

Ortis and the Salt Cod Barrel

A short walk from home, just the other side of the Arsenale, Venice's historic and current naval headquarters, is one of my favorite *alimentari* (the Italian word for convenience store). It is called Ortis and the shopfront alone is reason enough to visit. It has such beautiful, and unique, lettering on its marble fascia that I've tried to imagine all the characters in full with the vague ambition of one day creating a typeface. It's also a dairy, a *latteria*, and the two "t's" carved into the marble façade have such distinctive high bars that I first thought it said "lalleria"—a nonsense word in Italian.

But the reason this place is such a mecca is that it is the only shop left in Venice where *baccalà mantecato* is made on the premises. Admittedly, the practice stops in warm weather, but from October to March, the barrels outside the shop contain salt cod in various stages of soaking and desalination. From what I have observed, the cod makes its way up the sections of the barrel as the white-coated shop assistants move it every few hours to cleaner water, softening and desalting the delicate flesh. Then, the old fellows (none can be much younger than seventy) whip the flaked cod with parsley, garlic, and olive oil until it reaches that gorgeous, fluffy consistency so beloved in the region (see page 232).

Baccalà mantecato is such an important dish in the Venetian canon. Its history is almost as tasty as the dish itself. Pietro Querini, a Venetian nobleman of the fifteenth century, was sailing to Flanders when storms almost destroyed his ship. He reached a small island in the Norwegian archipelago of Lofoten, where he and his crew spent four months while the ship was repaired. During this time, he became so enamored with the local dried cod and the way it was softened and spiced that he began importing it when back in Venice.

At Ortis, it is the classic *mantecato* that is made, but the variation from Vicenza—*vicentina*—is equally popular (see page 233) and I've even come across a red version made with a tomato sauce. The shop is a tiny time capsule and I get the impression that not much has changed in the last eighty years or so.

PORK IN MILK

For 6

Most Italian main course dishes come complete and do not require accompanying bowls of vegetables, rice, or french fries. This has something to do with the classic meal structure in Italy: antipasti (starters), primi (pasta course), secondi (main course), dolci (desserts). When you are eating four courses, you don't need to bulk out the main dish. In fact, you will almost certainly feel overfull if you do.

This delicate, tender dish, then, should be enjoyed simply and preferably on its own. Just a couple of medium thick slices with a fairly generous amount of the milky sauce always does the trick.

¼ cup (½ stick) butter
1 clove of garlic, peeled and bashed
2¼ pounds lean, boneless porklion, trussed
1 bay leaf
1 sprig of rosemary
 a small handful of sage

ground cinnamon
flaky sea salt
freshly ground black pepper
4¼ cups whole milk, plus more for
 topping up

Take a heavy, lidded casserole dish and melt the butter over medium heat. Add the garlic, then put in the pork and brown each side. Throw in the bay leaf, rosemary, sage, a small pinch of cinnamon, a good pinch of salt, and a twist of black pepper.

Meanwhile, heat the milk in a separate saucepan and, when it starts to foam, pour it over the pork. Reduce the heat to low, and place the lid askew on the casserole dish to let steam escape. Simmer for 1½ to 2 hours, basting occasionally and adding more milk a little at a time if it dries out.

Remove the pork and place it on a chopping board. Cover loosely with a sheet of foil and rest it for 15 minutes. The milk, meanwhile, will appear thick, dark golden brown, and textured. This is normal. Turn the heat up to medium under the casserole dish and, using a wooden spoon, scrape all the sticky bits from the bottom of the pan and stir vigorously. If the liquid is too stiff or scant, add a splash or two of water. Strain through a sieve into a small saucepan, test the seasoning and adjust if necessary, bring to a boil for a minute, then remove from the heat.

The pork will be nicely tender by now. Remove the string and, using a very sharp knife, slice thinly, laying the meat on warmed plates. Spoon over a generous amount of the sauce and pour the rest into a small jug, to place on the table.

PORK RIBS *with* CABBAGE

For 4

Each of the morning pit stops along Via Garibaldi—the butcher, the greengrocer, the fishmonger, the lottery ticket shop, the caffè—provides a fresh opportunity for the locals to gossip and swap news. They perform an essential role in keeping the neighborhood together. As an outsider, I could never hope to be welcomed fully into the fold (my grasp of Venetian dialect is rudimentary, to say the least), but some of my neighbors are occasionally willing to share cooking tips and recipes with me; it is well known that the Englishman is here to cook.

This preparation of ribs is somewhat counterintuitive, since conventional wisdom is that they require the grill or the oven to loosen the tight flesh, but it is a lovely stew made very inexpensively with cheap pork ribs, described enthusiastically to me one morning by Mrs. Scarpa's seventy-five-year-old boy toy.

extra virgin olive oil
8 pork ribs
2 large onions, sliced
flaky sea salt
1 clove of garlic, peeled and finely sliced

1 large Savoy cabbage
sherry vinegar
¾ cup plus 2 tablespoons chicken stock (see page 304)
freshly ground black pepper

Heat a couple of tablespoons of olive oil in a large frying pan and brown the ribs on all sides. Make sure they have a nice, deep golden brown color. Drain the chops of oil and fat and set aside.

In a separate large pan for which you have a lid, heat a good glug of oil and gently sauté the sliced onions with a pinch of salt. Keep the heat low and continue to soften for about 5 minutes, until glossy and translucent. Add the garlic and sauté for a further minute or two, still on a low heat, so that nothing takes on color.

Meanwhile, remove the tough core of the cabbage and slice the leaves very thinly. Wash and dry them, then add to the pan of onions. Stir a few times to coat the cabbage leaves and incorporate the onions. Turn up the heat, continuing to stir occasionally, then add a good splash of vinegar. Within a few seconds this will start to evaporate; when this happens, add the stock. Stir, adding a pinch of salt and a good twist of black pepper. When it is bubbling nicely, place the ribs in the pan, reduce the heat, cover with the lid, and cook for an additional 8 to 10 minutes on a low simmer.

Serve in shallow bowls, with a few slices of grilled polenta (see page 171).

SALTIMBOCCA

For 4

There are certain classic dishes within the canon of Italian cooking that are there to make you look good. Part of the joy of feeding other people, whether you are a professional chef or a home cook, is receiving their praise and approbation.

I always find saltimbocca an easy win. It looks so impressive, appears deceptively complex, as if some great skill has gone into its preparation and execution, but the truth is that it is a cinch. It is also one of those dishes for which you are permitted to make a lot of noise in the kitchen. As you are flattening the veal with a rolling pin, it is legitimate to sound as though you're building a shed.

Veal, by the way, does not need to be cooked through, so do not leave the cutlets in the pan too long. Better to take them out sooner rather than later, rest them, and concentrate on making that delicious lemon and Marsala reduction.

4 medium veal cutlets
8 sage leaves
8 slices of prosciutto
⅔ cup "00" flour, seasoned

extra virgin olive oil
a large knob of butter
a large glass of Marsala
1 lemon, halved

Lay the cutlets on a large, clean work surface and, using a heavy wooden rolling pin or a smooth wooden mallet, bash them several times, with gusto, until they are around ¼-inch thick.

Place two sage leaves on each cutlet, wrap with prosciutto, using 2 slices per cutlet, and push together with your hands. Dust evenly with a little seasoned flour.

Place a large, heavy-bottomed frying pan over medium heat and warm a good glug of olive oil. Add the butter, and when it is starting to froth, fry the veal for 3 to 4 minutes on each side, until the prosciutto is crisp and golden brown. Remove to a warmed plate and turn the heat up under the pan. Add the Marsala, allow it to bubble up, scrape the sticky burned bits from the bottom, and reduce the sauce to a syrupy consistency. Squeeze in the juice of one of the lemon halves, and cut the other half into quarters.

Serve the veal with a generous drizzle of the Marsala sauce, a lemon wedge, and a crunchy radicchio salad.

SLOW-ROASTED VEAL SHIN

For 6

The reason slow-roasted meats appeal so much in these cold, dark months is that they become a focus for the day and take our minds away from the gloaming and our depleted levels of serotonin. This veal shin roast is a perfect example.

1 small whole veal shin, approx. 4½ pounds
extra virgin olive oil
flaky sea salt
freshly ground black pepper
a glass of white wine
4¼ cups veal stock
1 bay leaf

2 whole cloves of garlic, peeled
1 lemon
a small handful of sage
a small handful of thyme
¼ cup (½ stick) butter
plain flour

Remove the veal shin from the fridge 30 minutes before you start your preparation, to make sure it is at room temperature. Set the oven to 325°F/160°C.

Place the veal in a roasting pan and generously smother with olive oil, using your hands to rub it in and coat completely. Liberally sprinkle with salt and black pepper. Add the wine to the roasting pan along with enough of the stock to create a shallow moat no deeper than ½-inch. Drop in the bay leaf and garlic. Cut the lemon in two, squeeze the juice into the pan and drop in the halves. Crush the herbs in your hand and scatter them evenly over and around the shin. Using thick, good quality foil, tightly cover the pan and place in the oven.

Roast for 1¼ hours, checking once or twice to make sure the meat isn't drying out. Add more stock as necessary.

Remove the foil (but don't throw it away), then increase the oven to 400°F/200°C and roast the veal for another half an hour or so, basting regularly. Carefully remove the shin, place on a large, warmed plate and loosely cover with the retained foil.

Put the roasting pan with all the juices and other remains over high heat, stirring vigorously with a fork, scraping the burned and sticky bits back into the sauce, adding a little more stock to create a hearty gravy. Add the butter and a tablespoon of flour, scattered slowly from a height to avoid clumping. Whisk enthusiastically. Pour the liquid through a sieve into a saucepan and keep it bubbling.

Now, using a very sharp knife, take long, thin slices from the rested shin, lay them on warmed plates, pour over the veal gravy, and serve with steamed and buttered cavolo nero.

VEAL CHOPS *with* SAGE *and* LEMON

For 4

Occasionally I will eat something in a restaurant that is so delicious, so memorable, and yet apparently simple, that I will attempt to unravel it, a little like trying to work out how a magician performs a trick.

This happened one evening at Antiche Carampane and the plate in question was a veal chop. What could be simpler? The sauce was a butter, lemon juice, and sage reduction. But the combination was sublime and I made a few notes so that I could try re-creating it at home.

Of course, when my mind had cleared the next day, I realized what I already knew: there was no art, there was no magic or sorcery. It was a simple case of using excellent ingredients combined with a modest amount of technique. The essence of Italian cooking.

So, choose superb quality, plump veal chops, and the ingredients will do the hard work for you.

extra virgin olive oil
4 veal loin chops, about the thickness
*   of your thumb*
plain flour, to coat
a small handful of sage leaves

flaky sea salt
freshly ground black pepper
1 lemon
a small glass of white wine
⅓ cup (¾ stick) butter

Heat a few good glugs of olive oil in a very heavy frying pan with deep sides over medium. Dust the chops with flour immediately before placing them in the hot pan with a scattering of sage leaves. Depending on the size of your pan, you may need to do this in batches. Brown the veal evenly on all sides, seasoning with salt and pepper as you go, turning frequently, cooking for around 6 minutes. Remove the chops, place them on top of each other on a warm plate to rest, but leave the pan on the stove.

Halve the lemon and squeeze the juice of one half into the pan. When the juice has almost evaporated, turn the heat up high and add the wine. This will bubble rapidly and produce a stunning aroma. Scrape all the sticky bits from the bottom of the pan to incorporate into the sauce. When it starts to look thick and syrupy, add the butter, stir vigorously for 30 seconds, and remove from the heat.

Lay a chop on each of four warmed plates, pour over the sage and lemon sauce, then cut the remaining lemon half into four long wedges and garnish.

ROAST LEG *of* LAMB *with* ANCHOVY *and* ROSEMARY

For 4 to 6

I have to admit, this is a cult recipe. I have seen and eaten versions of it everywhere and I make it often during the winter months for my Venetian friends. I was particularly delighted that it was requested one November by a chum for the feast of Maria della Salute instead of the more traditional castradina (see page 284).

There are two important notes I need to make. First, it is essential that you really pound the ingredients in the mortar to form a paste. This is pushed into the incisions you make in the lamb and will dissolve into the flesh during the cooking process. The smoother you make the paste, the deeper the flavor will penetrate. And second, you must rub the meat thoroughly with your hands to coat the leg and allow those pungent ingredients to glaze as it roasts.

This is a foolproof choice for a Sunday roast, by the way, and one that will fill the house with wonderful cooking aromas.

4½ pounds of lamb leg
2 cloves of garlic, peeled
a large handful of rosemary, stalks removed
freshly ground black pepper
flaky sea salt
2 small cans of anchovy fillets in olive oil
a glass of white wine

Remove the lamb from the fridge half an hour before starting your preparation. Preheat the oven to 350°F/180°C.

Roughly chop the garlic and place in a large mortar with half the rosemary, a hearty twist of pepper, and a very good pinch or two of salt. Open one of the cans of anchovies and place them, oil and all, in the mortar. Pound enthusiastically with the pestle for a few minutes, until you have a rough paste. Set aside.

Take a very sharp knife with a point and make half a dozen 1½-inch-deep incisions into the lamb leg at even intervals. Place it in a large, deep-sided roasting pan. Work the holes open a little with your fingers. Now push a teaspoonful of the paste into each hole with a single anchovy from the second can and an equal amount of the remaining rosemary. Pour any leftover oil from the mortar on top of the lamb leg and rub all over with your oily hands. Pour half the wine into the bottom of the pan.

Cover tightly with heavy-duty foil and place in the oven for 30 minutes. Remove the foil (but don't throw it away) and baste the lamb with its juices, then turn the oven up to 400°F/200°C and roast for an additional 45 minutes or so, until golden brown. Remove the leg, place on a board, and cover loosely with the retained foil. Rest for at least 15 minutes.

Place the roasting pan over high heat and get the juices bubbling, scraping the sticky bits from the bottom and sides. Add the remaining wine and reduce the liquid for a few minutes until syrupy and rich. Pour into a warmed sauceboat.

Slice the lamb and serve with the sauce at the table. This goes rather well with Venetian potatoes (see page 200).

CASTRADINA

For 4

As far as I can tell, this dish is eaten only once a year on November 21 for the festival of Maria della Salute. It is a celebration to commemorate the delivery of the city from a particularly prolonged and deadly episode of the plague. It's a beautiful occasion with a deep sense of local pride and custom, unlike the festival of Redentore in July, which feels more like a tourist event. The festivities in November include the building of a temporary bridge across the Grand Canal connecting the Basilica to the church of Salute.

Traditionally, castradina is made with castrated lamb, but you can also use regular lamb. The stew is a perfect slow-cooked winter warmer, and like many one-pot dishes it improves with age, so it is definitely worth making a large batch and reheating the leftovers the next day.

3¼ quarts beef stock
extra virgin olive oil
2 large onions, sliced
2 large waxy potatoes, peeled and cubed
flaky sea salt
freshly ground black pepper

1¾ pounds castrated (or regular) lamb
*   rump cut into very large cubes*
¼ cup (½ stick) butter
2 celery stalks, chopped
1 clove of garlic, chopped
1 Savoy cabbage, cored and sliced

First, bring the beef stock up to a boil in a large pot, then reduce to a steady simmer.

Take a large casserole dish with a lid, heat a few glugs of olive oil, and sauté half the sliced onions over medium heat for 5 minutes. Add the potato cubes, a very good pinch of salt and a twist of pepper. Stir for an additional couple of minutes. Add the cubes of lamb and gently turn them around the casserole until they are starting to brown. Now add most of the stock, retaining a small cupful, bring to a boil, stir, then reduce to a low simmer and position the lid askew, leaving a little space for the steam to escape. Simmer for 2½ hours, stirring once or twice.

Meanwhile, in a separate heavy pan, melt the butter over medium heat and sauté the remaining onions until soft and glossy. Add the celery, garlic, and cabbage, with a good pinch of salt, and continue to cook for an additional 5 minutes. Add the retained cup of beef stock, cover, then reduce the heat and stew for 40 minutes.

Put the casserole of *castradina* on a heatproof tile in the middle of the table with a ladle, several warmed bowls, and the stewed cabbage.

BAKED STUFFED ONIONS

For 4

There are so many different types of onion available on the market stalls at Rialto, and even at the floating greengrocer at the top of Via Garibaldi, that I sometimes go a bit rabbit-in-headlights when choosing. I have a particular fondness for the pearly white variety, perfect for when you need to melt your onions for making silky smooth sauces, bigoli in salsa or sarde in saor, for example. Red onions are great when used very thinly sliced and raw in salads. The delightfully tiny cipollini are perfect for soups and stews.

But it is the common-or-garden variety that is required here, the type with yellow flesh and a thick, brown skin and, thankfully, available just about anywhere. It's a robust vegetable, sweet when cooked and firm enough to hold its shape nicely even when stuffed and baked.

8 large onions, peeled but intact
4 large herby Italian sausages
extra virgin olive oil
4 tablespoons breadcrumbs
a handful of pine nuts, roughly crushed
4 tablespoons grated Parmesan

1 large egg
a pinch of ground cinnamon
a small handful of picked thyme leaves
flaky sea salt
freshly ground black pepper

Preheat the oven to 350°F/180°C.

Bring a large pan of salted water to a gentle boil and plunge the onions in for no more than 5 minutes. Remove, drain, and allow to cool.

Take each sausage and carefully cut the skin lengthwise. Push the meat out onto a plate and discard the skins. Heat a glug of olive oil in a frying pan and crumble in the sausage meat. Sauté until brown, using a wooden spatula to break up the meat and keep a loose consistency. Transfer the meat from the pan onto paper towels and allow to rest.

Place the breadcrumbs, pine nuts, Parmesan, egg, cinnamon, and half the thyme in a large mixing bowl and combine everything thoroughly with a wooden spoon. Add the sausage meat. Mix again. Loosen with a little glug of olive oil and season generously with salt and black pepper.

Using a very sharp serrated knife, carefully slice the top off each onion and scoop out the center to create a cavity about the size of a large walnut. Stuff the sausage meat mixture equally into each, place the onions on a baking sheet, lightly coat with olive oil, and scatter over the remaining thyme and a few crunches of flaky salt. Bake in the oven for 25 to 30 minutes.

GRILLED RADICCHIO

For 4

There are two other principal types of radicchio besides the flower-like Treviso tardivo: the round variety known as Chioggia, and the torpedo-shaped Treviso. While the second is the most common and certainly the best known in international food markets, it's the other two that feature most prominently in Venetian kitchens. They are adored in northern Italy because they satisfy that distinctive bitter flavor profile so necessary in the region's cooking.

When grilled, a little of that bitterness is tempered somewhat and miraculously becomes almost sweet, so you end up with one of the classic, and most prized, Italian flavor combinations, agrodolce. These are wonderful when grilled, by the way; so dense and meaty that I will happily eat them as an alternative to steak.

4 small heads of Treviso radicchio
extra virgin olive oil
flaky sea salt
freshly ground black pepper
a small handful of flat parsley leaves, finely chopped

Remove and discard the stalk from the individual radicchio heads and slice each into quarters, lengthwise.

Place them into a very large mixing bowl and coat generously with olive oil and plenty of salt and pepper. Using your hands, turn the radicchio heads over enthusiastically to ensure they are fully coated.

Place a grill pan over high heat and, one by one, shaking off excess oil first, grill the radicchio on all sides, several minutes per piece, making sure they benefit fully from the heat and attain grill lines and charred edges. Carefully set aside each as you go.

When all the radicchio is grilled, divide equally among four plates, scatter over the chopped parsley, and serve with a little bowl of flaky sea salt.

VENETIAN MANHATTAN

For 1

The classical music concerts that one sees advertised in the churches and concert halls of Venice tend to be touristy affairs with familiar program of popular chamber music, sometimes with the musicians dressed in seventeenth-century costume. Not my cup of tea, I'm afraid.

There are, of course, exceptions. I attended a wonderful recital in a small room at the Conservatorio di Musica just off Campo San Stefano. It was effectively a concert of Baroque B-sides. At a reception held afterward, this delicious variation on a classic Manhattan, using Vecchia Romagna instead of rye whiskey, was served. Additionally, the garnish was an Amarena wild cherry from Modena. It was such a great drink that I quizzed the bartender and made notes of the recipe, which I reproduce here.

1 tablespoon sweet vermouth
¼ cup Vecchia Romagna

Angostura bitters
1 Amarena cherry (and a few drops of the syrup)

Fill a cocktail shaker with ice and pour in the sweet vermouth and the Vecchia Romagna. Add a few splashes of Angostura bitters and ½ teaspoon of Amarena cherry syrup. Using a long-handled bar spoon, stir enthusiastically for 20 seconds, then strain into an elegant cocktail glass. Garnish with a single Amarena cherry, preferably with stalk still attached.

ESPRESSO *and* SAMBUCA GRANITA

For 6

In order for this delicious granita to work, you really do need an intense coffee flavor. I find that filter coffee, no matter how many scoops you put in, produces a weak and unsatisfying result. Bialetti moka stovetop coffee makers are better, as long as you use strong, espresso-style grounds. This is a perfect little dolce for those, like me, who can't always manage a pudding after a meal.

12 double espressos (about 2¾ cups)
½ cup superfine caster sugar

¼ cup sambuca
6 mint leaves

Make sure the coffee is hot. Use the most intense grading of brewed coffee if you haven't got access to an espresso machine. Dissolve the sugar in the coffee and add the sambuca.

Allow the mixture to cool completely and transfer to a metal bowl. Place in the freezer for 45 minutes. Remove, whisk with a fork until slushy, and return to the freezer for 45 minutes. Repeat this three more times, making sure the mixture is fully slushed each time.

Freeze for a final 45 minutes to an hour before serving. Loosen with a spoon, divide equally among six pretty, chilled glasses and garnish with a mint leaf.

FRITOLE (VENETIAN DOUGHNUTS)

Makes 20 or so

After the celebrations of Christmas and the New Year, Venice can feel a little drab and empty. Many of the good restaurants close, and a lot of residents spend time with their extended families on the mainland. The days are cold and short and January in particular feels like a month that is neither here nor there. Thank god, then, for doughnuts.

In the run-up to carnevale (always on, before, and beyond Shrove Tuesday) the caffès, bakeries, and cake shops start to make fritole, typically Venetian street doughnuts, a tradition that goes back centuries. They are uneven and clumsy, packed with fruit and covered with sugar, but incredibly moreish and essential with my morning coffee. It's the best way I know to get through the winter blues.

½ cup superfine sugar
2 packets of dried yeast (½ ounce)
4 cups "00" flour
2 medium eggs, whisked
whole milk

¾ cup sultanas
1 teaspoon lemon zest
1 teaspoon orange zest
fine salt
4¼ cups vegetable oil, for deep-frying

Dissolve a teaspoon of sugar in a cup of warm water and stir in the dried yeast. Place the flour in a very large mixing bowl and, using a wooden spoon, stir in the eggs, ⅓ cup of the sugar and the yeast water. Now, continuing to stir, add enough milk a little at a time to create a soft and loose dough. Add the sultanas, the zests, and a pinch of salt, mix thoroughly until the dough is pliable and springy, then cover with a damp cloth or plastic wrap and leave in a warm place for 2 hours.

When the dough has risen, probably to double its original size, heat the vegetable oil to around 375°F/190°C in a large saucepan. You can test this by dropping a small cube of white bread in the pan—it should turn golden brown in 20 seconds.

Scoop out a dessertspoonful of the dough at a time and drop into the hot oil. Make sure you don't crowd the pan. The doughnuts should start to turn golden after a couple of minutes. Turn them over with a slotted spoon for another couple of minutes on the other side (5 to 6 minutes in total), then remove from the oil onto several sheets of paper towels. While they are still hot, sprinkle with the remaining sugar and serve immediately, or set aside in a warm place and serve at room temperature when you are ready.

VENETIAN RICE PUDDING POTS

For 6

With so much emphasis placed on risotto in Italian cooking, it is easy to forget that the same raw material makes a superb dessert, too.

Rich, comforting, and fragrant, rice pudding tends to evoke childhood memories in me. My grandmother would often serve a large bowl straight from the oven. The brown, sugary skin was always the most coveted part of the dish and my brothers and I would squabble for the prize. These individual pots allow each of you to have your own pudding skin (without fighting).

a small handful of raisins
¼ cup amaretto
2 cups whole milk
1 cup Arborio rice
1 cinnamon stick
1 vanilla pod

1 ¾ cups single cream
¾ cup superfine sugar
the zest of 1 orange
7 ounces mascarpone
2 tablespoons flaked almonds
2 tablespoons demerara or brown sugar

Soak the raisins in the amaretto for an hour.

Put the milk and rice into a large saucepan with the cinnamon stick. Scrape the seeds out of the vanilla pod and add those, too. Place over medium heat and bring to a boil, then reduce to a simmer. Allow to bubble gently for about half an hour, stirring frequently with a wooden spoon, until the milk has been mostly absorbed.

Now add the cream, the superfine sugar, the orange zest, stir in the drained raisins. Increase the heat a little until you see a bubble or two, then reduce to a simmer and cook for an additional half an hour, stirring occasionally.

Remove from the heat, take out the cinnamon stick, stir in the mascarpone, and allow the tender, creamy rice to cool a little. Turn on the broiler to a medium-high setting or preheat the oven to 400°F/200°C.

Divide the rice pudding between six 1-cup ovenproof ramekins. Crush the flaked almonds roughly between your finger and thumb and distribute evenly on top of the rice. Scatter an equal amount of demerara sugar on each. Transfer the ramekins to a baking sheet and place under the broiler or in the oven for a few minutes, until the almonds have turned golden brown and the sugar is starting to caramelize. (The oven method will take slightly longer than the broiler.)

Remove and allow to cool slightly before serving with a delicate teaspoon. Warn your guests that the ramekins may still be hot.

P A N T R Y

"True gastronomy is making the most of what is available, however modest." *Claudia Roden*

Living in Venice has taught me to be a better shopper. In a large city like London, where there are few convenient centralized markets, the grocery run tends to be weekly, and usually from one supermarket. This forces you to plan an entire six days ahead and to perform a mental juggling act with best-before dates, shelf life, and fridge space. Shopping the Venetian way, which is taking a wheeled shopping basket to the grocer, butcher, and fishmonger every morning, forces a better understanding of ingredients, seasonality, and household management. Most of my neighbors, me included, have no idea what to cook on a particular day, until the morning shop has been done. Produce dictates the menu, not the other way around.

But it's not all about the fresh stuff. Many traditional Venetian dishes predate refrigeration and so have inventive means of preservation. This might be marinating fish in vinegar and onions, as in the classic *in saor* (sweet and sour) preparation (see page 122), or using heavily salted goods such as salt cod for the delicious *baccalà mantecato* (page 232). But a simpler way to a happy kitchen is having a substantial supply of dried and canned food, in other words, a well-stocked pantry.

The definition of a store-pantry recipe is one that can be made at home without going to the market or the shops. In other words, the contents of your fridge and pantry should be able to furnish your home-cooking repertoire with several tasty dishes without you needing to change out of your pajamas.

There are two separate flanks to a good pantry strategy. On the one hand, you need to have a small arsenal of long-life essentials. I have so many cans of chickpeas, anchovies, jars of olives, and packets of lentils and dried mushrooms that I feel fairly confident I could survive a zombie apocalypse. On the other hand, Italian cooking requires certain staples and it is to these that this chapter turns its attention.

By the way, I would never be so presumptuous as to tell you what you need in your pantry—only you will be able to decide what works best for you—but if you don't have decent quantities of dried pasta, risotto rice, canned anchovies, and onions, you are asking for trouble. You might be surprised at that last item: onions. Surely they are greengrocery? Not so. Onions are so essential to Venetian home cooking, and to my personal kitchen preferences, that I panic somewhat if I don't have at least a couple pounds at any one time. They sit quite happily in a cool cupboard and they last for such a long time that I think of onions as a pantry staple as well as fresh produce.

A VIBRANT SPRING PESTO

Makes about ¾ cup

I still buy jars of good-quality pesto from the supermarket for those occasions when I need a quick meal with zero preparation. But when confronted with a massive bunch of basil on a spring morning at the greengrocer, my first thought is to make my own.

Basil has such an intense aroma, heady and narcotic. You want the very largest leaves, almost fleshy, and you should discard the stalks. This pesto is so fresh and zingy it will liven up pretty much anything. I love it with strozzapretti pasta or in a simple white risotto.

¼ cup pine nuts • 2 large handfuls of basil leaves, roughly chopped • ½ a clove of garlic, finely chopped • flaky sea salt • freshly ground black pepper • extra virgin olive oil • ⅓ cup grated Parmesan

Dry-fry the pine nuts in a large, heavy pan over high heat for a few minutes until *just* starting to color, no more. Set aside to cool.

Put the basil leaves, garlic, a pinch of salt, twist of pepper, and a good glug or two of olive oil into a food processor; pulse briefly. Turn the processor on and add more olive oil in a steady thin stream until you have a wet paste. Add most of the grated Parmesan.

Roughly crush the pine nuts in a mortar and pestle. Transfer to a medium mixing bowl with the basil mix. Add the remaining Parmesan and more olive oil if necessary. Try to end up with a glossy paste with a rustic consistency. Store in an airtight container in the fridge.

SALSA VERDE

Makes about 1 cup

I hate waste in the kitchen and will go into a bit of a decline if there is an ingredient I can't save or use before it expires, wilts, goes off, or dies. Parsley tends to get tired very quickly in hot weather, so if I find I have an abundance, I will make a batch of this versatile sauce. It is an excellent means of reincarnating parsley and giving it another two weeks of life.

It's a wonderfully pungent sauce to perk up grilled fish (and often boiled meat in Venice) and lends a glorious green glow to otherwise drab colors.

a small handful of breadcrumbs (see page 300) • 2 tablespoons red wine vinegar • 2 very large handfuls of flat parsley leaves • 1 heaping tablespoon small capers • 3 good anchovies, from a can • 1 small clove of garlic, very finely chopped • ½ cup extra virgin olive oil

Put the breadcrumbs and vinegar into a small bowl, turn over once, and leave for 10 minutes. Meanwhile, chop the parsley leaves, the capers, and the anchovies and put them into a very large mortar. Add the garlic and, using a fork, mix the ingredients together.

Now mash everything together with the pestle, making sure the chopped anchovy does not clump. Slowly stir in the olive oil, incorporating all the ingredients into a loose green paste.

Store in an airtight container in the fridge for up to a week until needed, but stir thoroughly before using.

BREADCRUMBS

Makes about 6 cups—that's 5 "large" handfuls or 8 "small" handfuls

There are some kitchen chores that I really enjoy, and making breadcrumbs is one of them. This is partly because, before decamping to Venice, I would not have dreamed of making my own—I would've picked up a packet of Japanese panko at the supermarket. But Italian home cooks don't waste anything, and there is a minor sense of achievement watching the metamorphosis of an inedible hunk of stale bread into a versatile ingredient with an impressive shelf life.

½ a loaf of old bread—2 or 3 days is perfect • extra virgin olive oil

Preheat the oven to 325°F/160°C.

Tear the bread into small chunks and scatter on a baking sheet with a liberal drizzling of olive oil. Turn over with your hand a few times to coat every piece.

Place in the oven for 5 to 6 minutes, until just turning golden. Shake the tray to turn the pieces and return to the oven for a few minutes more. The bread should not be too brown but should have a good, crisp crunch.

Remove and allow to cool. Transfer to a large bowl, crush roughly with the back of a wooden spoon or your fingers, and transfer to an airtight container. They will keep for up to a week.

TOMATO SAUCE

For 4

No need to overcomplicate this. It's an easy vegetarian classic that goes well with anything. Leave it chunky as a *ragù* for pasta, or blend it to make a superb smooth tomato sauce for meatballs. It will keep in the fridge for at least a week. The key is to chop the *soffritto* (that's the Italian word for finely chopped onion, carrot, and celery) as finely as possible and soften it slowly before adding the tomatoes.

extra virgin olive oil • 1 large onion, finely chopped • 1 large carrot, finely chopped • 1 large celery stalk, finely chopped • 1 clove of garlic, finely chopped • 2 × 14-ounce cans of chopped Italian tomatoes • 2 tablespoons passata (tomato purée) • a small handful of basil leaves, torn • 1 bay leaf • flaky sea salt • freshly ground black pepper

Heat a good few glugs of olive oil in a large pan. Sauté the onion, carrot, celery, and garlic over medium heat for 10 minutes, until soft and glossy. Do not brown. Add the tomatoes and passata and stir well. Now add the basil, bay leaf, and a very good pinch of salt and pepper.

Turn the heat to low, cover, and simmer for 40 minutes, stirring occasionally. You may need to add a splash or two of water if the sauce is too stiff—you want it to be loose and shiny. Test the seasoning and remove the bay leaf.

PIZZA DOUGH

Makes 6 × 10-inch pizzas

I am always wary of recipes that claim to be foolproof. You never know how foolish others might be. However, this recipe for pizza dough is so consistently reliable that it has never gone wrong. My youngest daughter, Mabel, has been making this successfully since the age of seven.

*4 cups very strong white bread flour
(in Italy it is always "00" flour) •
2 teaspoons fine salt • ¼ ounce (1 packet)
easy-bake yeast • extra virgin olive oil*

On a large, clean work surface, carefully put the flour into a small mound and evenly mix in the salt and the yeast. (You could do this in a bowl, of course, but in Italian domestic kitchens I have never seen it done any other way than on the worktop.)

Make a well in the middle. Add about a tablespoon of olive oil and about ¾ cup plus 2 tablespoons warm water from a measuring jug of 2½ cups. Evenly bring the flour in from the walls of the well and slowly mix into a firm dough. Add more warm water, a little at a time, kneading and mixing all the while. You should not need to use all the remaining 1¾ cups of warm water, and make sure you do not make the dough too wet. When you have a thick, firm dough with a smooth consistency, continue to knead for an additional 10 to 12 minutes, pulling back and pushing forward.

If you prod your dough it should spring back slightly. Roll it into a ball, put it into a large bowl, cover it with oiled plastic wrap, and leave it in a warm place for 2 to 3 hours, until it has doubled in size.

When you are ready to make your pizzas, remove the now alarmingly large dough ball, knock it back down to size on a floured work surface, divide it into 6 equal parts, and roll into separate balls. You should be left with 6 balls around the same size as satsumas. The dough will keep in the fridge for up to 12 hours but you must remember to remove it half an hour before you want to use it.

GREMOLATA

Makes about 2 tablespoons

Gremolata is so easy to make that there is a strong argument for it never to be prepared in advance—making it at the last minute, as required, will strengthen its credentials and ensure it is always fresh and pungent. I use an old-school *hachoir* with wooden handles and rock the blade back and forth over the chopping board until the ingredients are extremely fine. Gremolata is brilliant for adding a zesty edge to fish and seafood.

*½ a clove of garlic, very finely chopped •
the zest of 1 lemon • a small handful
of flat parsley, very finely chopped*

Make sure you really have chopped everything very finely indeed. Put the ingredients into a small bowl and mix together. Use immediately.

FRESH PASTA IDEAL
FOR RAVIOLI
Enough for 4

There is, I am afraid, no such thing as a universal recipe for pasta. Every kitchen in Italy will have a slightly varied method and, furthermore, different uses will require different ingredients and techniques. Ravioli, for example, benefits greatly from pasta made with semolina as well as flour.

When rolling this pasta, use a large, flat wooden pin and create sheets as wide as possible. I try to make my ravioli big but still retaining the delicacy afforded by a thin layer of pasta.

2⅓ cups "00" flour, plus extra for dusting •
⅔ cup semolina • 2 large eggs,
plus 3 large yolks

Combine the two flours in a large mixing bowl. Deposit the mixed flours onto a large, clean work surface and make a well in the middle. If your work surface is too small, leave the flour in the bowl. Briefly whisk the eggs and extra yolks in a jug and pour them into the well. With a fork or wooden spoon, work around the inner edges of the well, carefully bringing all the flour into the middle to create wet lumps.

Using your fingers, combine the clumped dough and, adding a little more of the extra "00" flour if necessary (or flouring the work surface if you have been using a bowl up to this point), work the mixture into a ball. Knead the ball by pushing, pulling, and flattening—a bit like making bread but with a little less vigor—for around 6 minutes,

until the dough is smooth, shiny, and a little elastic. Add more flour if it is too sticky. (Add a couple of drops of cold water if it is too dry and has more than a few cracks.)

When the dough stops sticking to your hands, wrap the ball in plastic wrap and allow it to rest for at least half an hour. Alternatively, put it into the fridge to use later, where it will keep for up to 48 hours, but make sure you bring it back to room temperature before using.

When it has rested, your dough is ready to be unwrapped and rolled.

AN EASY FRESH PASTA
FOR SPAGHETTI, ETC.
Enough for 4

I have realized that the secret to really good pasta is having a large Carrara marble work surface. Many of the best unmodernized Venetian kitchens have exactly this and there is no better way to start the process— a mound of flour, a well for the egg yolks, and plenty of space to make a mess. If you don't have this in your kitchen, then improvise with the next best thing, even if it's a large chopping board on your kitchen table.

(By the way, if you want your pasta to have that gorgeous deep orange hue you sometimes see in professionally handmade fresh pasta in fancy stores, just add a teaspoon of passata (tomato purée). It makes all the difference to the color without being a detectable flavor. It's a trick I picked up from Francesco Zorzetto at La Cantina in Cannaregio.)

2¾ cups "00" flour, plus extra for dusting •
1 large egg, plus 4 large yolks

On a large, clean work surface, deposit the flour and make a well in the middle. If your work surface is too small, use a very large bowl instead. Briefly whisk the egg and yolks in a jug and pour them into the well. With a fork or wooden spoon, work around the inner edges of the well, slowly bringing all the flour into the middle to create wet, doughy lumps.

Using your hands, combine the clumped dough and, adding a little more flour if necessary (or flouring the work surface if you have been using a bowl up to this point), work the mixture into a ball. Knead the ball by pushing, pulling, and flattening—a bit like making bread but with a little less vigor—for around 6 minutes, until the dough is smooth, shiny, and a little springy. Add more flour if it is too sticky. (Add a couple of drops of cold water if it is too dry and has more than a few cracks.)

When the dough stops sticking to your fingers and palms, wrap the ball in plastic wrap and allow it to rest for at least half an hour. Alternatively, put it into the fridge to use later, where it will keep for up to 48 hours, but make sure you bring it back to room temperature before using. After resting, your dough is ready to be rolled.

SOFFRITTO

Makes about 12½ to 14 ounces (depending on the size of the onions and carrots)

This is the foundation stone of Italian cooking. It is what gives sauce ballast and soup integrity. It is also, in terms of its execution, the meditation at the start of a cooking session that puts me in the right frame of mind. I find the knife work and whittling down of the ingredients therapeutic and calming.

It is often worth making a batch of *soffritto* and keeping it uncooked in an airtight container in the fridge, particularly if you know you're going to be cooking for a few days on end or have guests staying.

2 large white onions • 2 large carrots • 1 celery stalk

Peel the onions and halve them, lengthwise, through the top and the root. Now, remove the top but leave the root end for the moment. Place the cut surface of the onion flat on the chopping board and slice back into the bulb with the knife parallel to the board. Now slice downward and lengthwise through the bulb to the board. Finally, cut across your long lacerations to create tiny cubes of onion, all the way up to the root, which you should then discard.

Peel the carrots, slice lengthwise into long matchsticks, then crosswise to make tiny cubes the same size as the onion pieces.

Peel the celery stalk to remove its stringy outer skin and repeat the method used for the carrots.

Combine the chopped ingredients and decant into a lidded container to put into the fridge for when you need it. *Soffritto* will keep for about 5 days.

VEGETABLE STOCK

Makes about 8½ cups

If I'm being honest, I have not seen a great deal of stock-making in the domestic kitchens of Venice. Sauces are usually loosened and flavored with pasta cooking water. However, I enjoy making this stock and it's a good way to use up vegetables that are looking a bit tired. Vegetable stock is excellent for light risottos and it makes soups a cinch.

*2 large onions, peeled and quartered •
2 celery stalks, quartered • 2 large
carrots, peeled and quartered • 1 large
leek, washed, trimmed, and quartered •
1 bay leaf • 1½ teaspoons fine salt*

Place all the ingredients in a stock pot. Add 3 cups of cold water and bring to a boil. Reduce to a simmer and allow to bubble gently for about an hour and a half, until reduced by a third.

Remove the scum from the surface, strain, and allow the stock to cool. Refrigerate until needed or freeze in small containers. It will keep in the fridge for 3 days or the freezer for 3 months.

AN EASY CHICKEN STOCK

Makes about 8½ cups

Absolutely every one of my neighbours, as far as I have been able to observe, uses cubes or bouillon when they need chicken stock, so you may do the same with my blessing, and the blessings of most of the residential population of eastern Venice.

This is an easy win, however, if you have eaten a roast chicken and want to extend its usefulness. Homemade chicken stock is superb in a hearty risotto or as a base for braised vegetables.

*1 or 2 chicken carcasses and bones from
legs and thighs • fine salt • 2 large onions,
peeled and quartered • 2 large carrots,
peeled and quartered • 1 celery stick,
quartered • 1 bay leaf*

Heat the oven to 350°F/180°C and roast the carcass(es) and bones in a roasting pan for 10 to 15 minutes. Remove from the oven. This is just to dry them out. It also helps intensify the flavor.

Put the carcass(es) and bones into a stockpot with about 3 quarts of cold water and a good pinch of salt and bring to a boil. Reduce to a bubbling simmer for about 15 minutes, then scrape the scum off the surface. Add the onions, carrots, celery, and bay leaf and continue to simmer gently for an additional 45 minutes, until reduced by a third.

Strain the stock and use immediately, refrigerate in a large airtight container for up to 4 days, or freeze in small batches and use within 3 months.

FISH STOCK
Makes about 8½ cups

The key to a good fish stock is delicacy and subtlety. It needs to be versatile and should not overpower the main ingredient for which it is used, but rather accompany and support it.

4½ pounds large fish heads and bones (your fish-monger will give you these free, usually) • fine salt • 2 large onions, peeled and quartered • 2 large carrots, peeled and quartered • 2 celery sticks, quartered

Put the fish heads and bones into a stock pot with about 3 quarts of cold water and a good pinch of salt and briefly bring to a boil. Reduce to a simmer for about 10 minutes, then scrape the scum off the surface. Add the onions, carrots, and celery, and continue to simmer gently for an additional 30 minutes, until reduced by a third.

Strain the stock and use immediately, refrigerate in a large airtight container for up to 4 days, or freeze in small batches and use within 3 months.

A RICH SEAFOOD STOCK
Makes about 6⅓ cups

A successful home cook in Venice can, and often will, get away without making stock, as I have mentioned in the other stock recipes. There is one exception, however, and that is seafood stock. Distinct from fish stock, which is much lighter, this is rich and intense. I often collect my shells when I'm dining out, requesting a bag to take home my shellfish detritus along with any other discards from the kitchen. You can freeze them until you need them.

extra virgin olive oil • 2¼ pounds shells from lobsters, prawns, crabs, crayfish, etc. • 1 large onion, quartered • 1 large carrot, quartered • 2 large celery stalks, quartered • 1 clove of garlic, halved • sea salt • a glass of white wine • 2 tablespoons passata (tomato purée) • 10½ cups hot water

In a stock pot, heat 3 tablespoons of olive oil over medium. Add the shells, the onion, carrot, celery, garlic, and a good pinch of salt, and stir. Turn the heat up a little until you get a gentle crackle. Continue to stir for a few minutes, until the shells and onions are starting to brown. When the shells begin to stick to the bottom of the pan, add the white wine. It will give off a satisfying hiss and a wonderfully pungent cloud of steam. Stir in the passata, bash the shells with a ladle, stir again, and add the hot water. Bring to the boil and allow to bubble up for 1 minute, then turn down the heat and simmer for about an hour, until the liquid has reduced by a third.

Carefully strain through a sturdy sieve into a separate large clean pan. This will make approximately 6 cups of deeply hued and aromatic stock, enough for two lots of the fish soup on page 160. Alternatively, it will keep, covered in the fridge, for 3 days or frozen in small batches for up to 2 months.

BIBLIOGRAPHY

Ackroyd, Peter, *Venice—Pure City* (Chatto & Windus, 2009)

Artusi, Pellegrino, *Science in the Kitchen and the Art of Eating Well*, 1891 (Marsilio, 1997)

Attlee, Helena, *The Land Where Lemons Grow* (Particular Books, 2014)

Boni, Giacomo, *The Lagoons of Venice* (Royal Institute of British Architecture, 1898)

Brodsky, Joseph, *Watermark* (Farrar, Straus & Giroux, 1992)

Brown, Horatio F., *Life on the Lagoons* (Rivington, Percival & Co, 1894)

Brusegan, Marcello, *La Cucina Veneziana* (Newton Compton, 2006)

Castelvetro, Giacomo (translated by Gillian Riley), *The Fruits, Herbs & Vegetables of Italy*, 1614 (Prospect Books, 1989)

Cipriani, Arrigo, *Harry's Bar—A Venetian Legend* (Alcione, 1996)

Coles, Polly, *The Politics of Washing* (Robert Hale, 2014)

Crowhurst Lennard, Suzanne H., *The Venetian Campo* (Corte del Fontego, 2012)

Damiani, Ludovica, *Set in Venice* (Electa, 2009)

David, Elizabeth, *Italian Food* (MacDonald, 1954)

Distefano, Giovanni, *How Was Venice Built?* (Supernova, 2014)

Fay, Stephen, and Knightly, Philip, *The Death of Venice* (André Deutsch, 1976)

Fenlon, Iain, *Piazza San Marco* (Profile Books, 2009)

Fletcher, Caroline, and da Mosto, Jane, *The Science of Saving Venice* (Umberto Allemandi, 2004)

Foscari, Giulia, *Elements of Venice* (Lars Müller, 2014)

Gransard, Marie-José, *Venice— A Literary Guide for Travellers* (I. B. Tauris, 2016)

Hazan, Marcella and Victor, *Ingredienti* (Scribner, 2016)

James, Henry, *Italian Hours* (Houghton, 1909)

Marías, Javier, *Venice, An Interior* (Penguin, 2016)

Matvejevi, Predrag, *The Other Venice* (Reaktion Books, 2007)

Morand, Paul, *Venices* (Pushkin Press, 2002)

Morris, Jan, *Venice* (Faber & Faber, 1960)

Norwich, John Julius, *A History of Venice* (Penguin, 1982)

Oliphant, Mrs., *The Makers of Venice* (Macmillan & Co, 1898)

Riley, Gillian, *The Oxford Companion to Italian Food* (Oxford University Press, 2007)

Ruskin, John, *The Stones of Venice Vol. I: The Foundations* (Smith, Elder & Co, 1853)

Ruskin, John, *The Stones of Venice Vol. II: The Sea Stories* (Smith, Elder & Co, 1853)

Ruskin, John, *The Stones of Venice Vol. III: The Fall* (Smith, Elder & Co, 1853)

Saikia, Robin, *The Venice Lido* (Somerset Books, 2011)

DIRECTORY

Restaurants

AL COVO
Calle de la Paescaria
Castello 3968
Vaporetto: Arsenale

ALLE TESTIERE
Calle del Mondo Novo
Castello 5801
Vaporetto: Rialto

ANTICHE CARAMPANE
Rio Terà de la Carampane
San Polo 1911
Vaporetto: San Silvestro

CÀ D'ORO ALLA VEDOVA
Calle Cà d'Oro
Cannaregio 3912
Vaporetto: Cà d'Oro

CORTE SCONTA
Calle del Pestrin
Castello 3886
Vaporetto: Arsenale

DAI TOSI
Calle Seco Marina
Castello 738
Vaporetto: Giardini

DALLA MARISA
Fondamenta S. Giobbe
Cannaregio 652
Vaporetto: Tre Archi

DA ROMANO
Via Baldassarre Galuppi
Burano 221
Vaporetto: Burano

LA BITTA
Calle Lunga de S. Barnaba
Dorsoduro 2753a
Vaporetto: Ca' Rezzonico

LA CANTINA
Campo San Felice
Cannaregio 3689
Vaporetto: Ca d'Oro

PARADISO PERDUTO
Fondamenta Misericordia
Cannaregio 2540
Vaporetto: Ca d'Oro

Bars, cafès, bàcari, gelateria

AL MERCA
Campo Bella Vienna
San Polo 213
Vaporetto: Rialto Mercato

ALL'ARCO
Calle dell'Ochialer
San Polo 436
Vaporetto: Rialto Mercato

CAFFÈ ROSSO
Campo Sta Margherita
Dorsoduro 2963
Vaporetto: Ca'Rezzonico

CANTINONE GIA SCHIAVI
Fondamenta Nani
Dorsoduro 992
Vaporetto: Accademia

I RUSTEGHI
Corte del Tentor
San Marco 5513
Vaporetto: Rialto

NICO
Fondamenta Zattere
Dorsoduro 922
Vaporetto: Zattere

ROSA SALVA
Campo SS. Giovanni e Paolo
Castello 6779
Vaporetto: Ospedale

My favorite grocery shop

ORTIS
Salizada Sta Giustina
Castello 2910
Vaporetto: San Zaccaria

My favorite bakery

RIZZARDINI
Campiello dei Meloni
San Polo 1415
Vaporetto: San Silvestro

My favorite bookshop

LIBRERIA ACQUA ALTA
Calle Longa Sta Maria Formosa
Castello 5176b
Vaporetto: Ospedale

I N D E X

ACKNOWLEDGMENTS

This book would not have been possible without the support and generosity of my wife Jules. Thank you for allowing me to spend so much time away from home. And thanks to my children Oliver, Martha, and Mabel for coming out to visit.

I am grateful to my brilliant editor Juliet Annan and her team at Penguin Fig Tree: Anna Steadman, Assallah Tahir, Poppy North, Sara Granger, Lindsay Terrell, Samantha Fanaken, Chantal Noel, Anjali Nathani, Catherine Wood, Lucy Beresford-Knox, and Annie Lee. Thanks also to Luke Crittenden.

John Hamilton and Sarah Fraser have made such a gorgeous book, and Jenny Zarins, once again, has captured the very essence of Venice and made the dishes look as beautiful as I could have hoped.

Thanks to Cathryn Summerhayes and Vanessa Fogarty at Curtis Brown, and to my dearest friend, Richard Beatty.

Anna Gerotto, Sarah Roberts, Signora Povinelli, and Signora Scarpa, who have all showed me more of Venice than I could ever have discovered on my own.

I owe a debt of gratitude to the following people for moral support on the ground, in Venice and beyond: John Hutton, Mark Hix, Angela Hartnett, Robin Hutson, Ewan Venters, Tom Parker Bowles, and Stephen and Flo Bayley.

I couldn't have done it without my friends in Venice, too: Luca and Bruno at Alle Testiere; Francesco, Matteo, and Anna at All'Arco; Giovanni at I Rusteghi; Alessandra and her sons at Cantinone già Schiavi; Francesco at Antiche Carampane; Jackie, Paolo, and Logan at Dai Tosi; and Francesco and Natasha at La Cantina. Additionally, thanks to Enrica Rocca, Anna Gilchrist, Martina and

I want to thank Jane da Mosto and her team at We Are Here Venice, an organization dedicated to protecting the city and the lagoon from rising sea levels, managing tourism, reversing the population decline, and banning multistory cruise ships. It is essential that Venice remains a living, breathing city for many generations to come. www.weareherevenice.org

This book is dedicated to my parents,

Carole Beadle and Cliff Norman.

I love you and I know that you have always loved me.

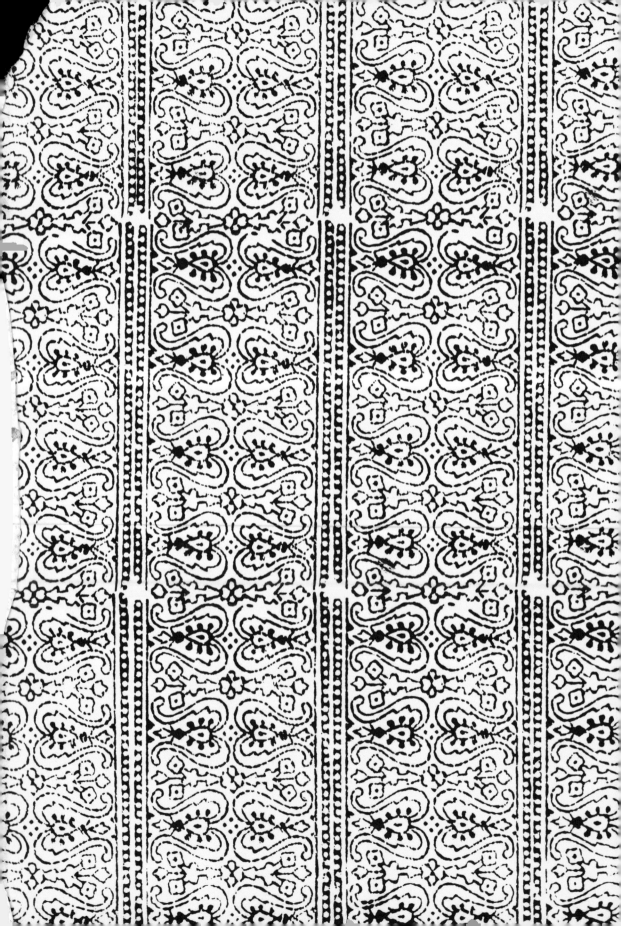